Nowhere like This Place

Nowhere like This Place

Tales from a Nuclear Childhood

Marilyn Carr

IGUANA

Copyright @ 2020 Marilyn Carr
Published by Iguana Books
720 Bathurst Street, Suite 303
Toronto, ON M5S 2R4

Cover image: Harold Toiviainen
Cover design: Meghan Behse

ISBN 978-1-77180-435-6 (paperback)
ISBN 978-1-77180-436-3 (epub)
ISBN 978-1-77180-437-0 (Kindle)

This is an original print edition of *Nowhere like This Place: Tales
from a Nuclear Childhood.*

For Debbie, Ruth, and Julie, three-quarters of the DRW.
There has never been a dull moment, and we are so not done yet.

1

This Must Be the Place

I am a girl between two boys. My older brother has just graduated from kindergarten and my younger brother has not yet graduated from diapers. Our two-tone green Mercury Meteor has bench seats and the subdued version of tail fins that signals the segue into the more streamlined 1960s automotive silhouette. All three of us kids are probably rattling around in the back. Seatbelts are not yet standard or even luxury equipment in 1958 Mercuries. My baby brother might actually be in the front seat wheel well in his bassinet, ready to become a compact projectile. Sometime in the near future, when we graduate to a Plymouth Valiant station wagon, my little brother will have a car seat that clips to the top of the bench, complete with a steering wheel and a horn. The horn is definitely not a good design feature, nor is the placement of the child seat. But that's not a hazard for today. We have plenty of other ones.

The speedometer probably goes all the way to seventy. The road sign suggests about half that and we're lucky to achieve the legal maximum on the downhills. We're headed west to Ontario in 1960 to my dad's new job at somewhere called "the plant." The moving van is a day behind us. If I were tall enough to see out the window, I would see an endless stretch of farmland with row upon row of bales of hay. It smells like cow doo-doo. "Fresh country air," my dad says, and he laughs uproariously like this is supposed to be funny. Like he hasn't said it about a hundred times since we got in the car.

We're emigrating from Quebec dairy country south of Montreal, where both my parents' families have lived since before Canada was born. I'm a little perplexed by the notion of moving since I don't remember moving before. I'm reluctantly along for the ride, like a cat in a travel carrier, cranky and complaining at first, then settling down into an uneasy truce with the inevitable and unknowable that comes with relocating to somewhere new.

My mother packed a lunch like she always does. There are no restaurants along the highway anyhow. We pull over to a rest stop with picnic tables and toilets. The toilets are the kind with wooden saloon doors and a gap between the roof and the wall to ensure maximum habitat for flies and spiders as big as dinner plates, at least as far as I'm concerned. If you choose the picnic table downwind from the "rest" facilities, it actually doesn't stink that bad.

My mother is a dietitian. After the oil cloth goes on the table and we all wash our hands from the hand pump at the well, a lunch covering all of the required food groups emerges. There are carrot and celery sticks, which we stick up our noses or turn into orange fangs. We do not eat them. There are probably bologna and mustard sandwiches on white bread with crusts and iceberg lettuce. I do not like bologna. My brother does not like crusts. The baby gums Cheerios and slobbers on the oil cloth. We drink water from the well pump that tastes like rust and smells like rotten eggs.

But at least it's fun to pump the water. Probably more water than strictly necessary. "You kids stop horsing around and acting like morons," Dad says.

There are hermit cookies full of raisins for dessert. You can squish them nicely in to a ball and the raisins will pop out. "You kids smarten up and stop playing with your food," Dad says. "And go to the bathroom. We're not stopping again." I do not go to the bathroom.

We stay at a motel for the night. The motel is just off the highway, as anonymous and innocuous as any other motel. Perhaps with one letter burned out: OTEL or MOTE. At certain times of the year there is probably a pool. Not this time of year. I've never been to a motel before. I'm concerned that our new house doesn't have a kitchen and I'll have to share a bed with my smelly brothers. This is not turning out very good.

We get to eat dinner at the diner. My grilled cheese sandwich has the right kind of orange cheese and squished crusts. My vanilla milkshake comes in a tall, V-shaped glass, and I also get the metal container from the milkshake machine with the bits that won't fit in the glass. My tongue would stick to it if I licked it but I know way better than that. It only takes once to know better than that. The milkshake is so thick it makes a really good slurping noise with the straw. I'm sure my dad wants to conjure up a Scotch. Or three or four Scotches.

We don't get to eat breakfast at the diner, though. My mother has packed breakfast. It's a Kellogg's Variety Pack of individual cereal packages. There are five of us and eight little boxes of breakfast, which would seem to be an appropriate abundance of choice. But a cereal variety pack has only one box of Frosted Flakes. One of my tactics is to pretend to want the Raisin Bran and hope my older brother will fight me over it so I'll end up with the Frosted Flakes. But even if he doesn't take the bait, Raisin Bran isn't that bad, because the raisins are covered in sugar. I open the fancy flap on the box and my mother pours in some milk. The milk makes the raisins rise to the top. I count three lousy raisins. I eat the raisins, let the bran flakes get soggy, then refuse to eat them. So there.

* * *

The town of Deep River is as brand new as it could possibly be. It was whacked out of the bush north of Algonquin Park in the wilds of Canada by German prisoners of war in 1944 to house the employees of the newly established Chalk River Nuclear Research Laboratories. Like my dad. And our nuclear family.

When we finally roll into town, our real new house is a blue bungalow. Beside a beige bungalow, beside a yellow bungalow, beside a white bungalow. It is barely fifteen years since the town sprang fully formed from the forest. The moving van arrives, along with our television set, although a reliable TV signal won't get there for another two years. If I were my mother, I'd be looking pretty grim.

Seventeen children swarm out of the seven houses on our curve of Newton Crescent. Having one child pretty much indicates you are just getting started. Only two children is a little stingy. Three is a good round number. Four is okay too, especially if there are twins in the mix. Five is pointing towards Catholicism. After that you are on your own.

We are as free range as organic hens. Everything outside our front doors is fair game for games. There are no fences between the yards and we flow from one to another as if through a porous pool of play. We are a whirl of arms and legs and striped t-shirts and pink skorts and scabby knees.

Tricycles and bicycles line the ditch like a freeway pileup, wheels still spinning as they are discarded for shinier objects.

We play vestigial games passed down in our parents' DNA. Kick the Can. Red Rover. Dodgeball. All of these involve running and grass stains and bruises and a distinct lack of adult supervision or intervention. Rules are made up on the fly and are never the same from day to day. Exactly the type of lessons that will come in handy when I enter the corporate world.

The vacant lot at the bottom of the crescent is covered in knee-high grass. That's where all the kids on our half of the street convene after dinner in the summer to play scrub baseball. I don't know who teaches us about scrub. We probably thought we invented it. And who could argue with that? I am really bad at scrub and always start out as a "cow." I also always end up as a cow. A cow hangs out in the outfield, waiting for a pop-fly or wayward ground ball that never shows up. A cow is so far in the outfield that by the time I make my way back to home plate at the end of the game, everyone is already in bed asleep.

* * *

There is a swamp at the end of our street. Not the kind of swamp you get in southern climates, with murky water teaming with amphibians that have a taste for human flesh. Ours is a Canadian Shield swamp with murky water teaming with insects that have a taste for human flesh. The swamp isn't even that swampy. Just swampy enough for cattails and muddy ooze and frogs the size of pennies known as spring peepers that we nickname roasty toasties due to their delightful tendency to explode like a kernel of popcorn when we strongly encourage them to jump into a campfire. But the swamp is more than swampy enough to be a cozy homestead for mosquitos.

There are attempts at various intervals to drain our neighbourhood swamp, but nature is having none of it. But not to worry. In the scheme of things, our swamp is only one of the many habitats pumping out blood-sport flies. There is no way we're going to outrun them so we have to outsmart them. Either that or decimate them. And that's where DDT comes in.

In the 1960s DDT is as wondrous as Wonder Bread. Not only for its impeccable poisonous prowess at bug and bald eagle control but also for the DDT fogging truck. Because that's how DDT launches its superpower into action. The fogging truck looks as innocuous as an ice cream truck, only it's industrial green. The driver has a white outfit but instead of a black bow tie and friendly milkman hat, he wears a white hood and a gas mask. This should have been our first clue.

The DDT truck doesn't need "Pop Goes the Weasel" to lure us in. All it needs to do is show up. In the manner of children everywhere, there is a telepathic connection between us. When we hear the silent jungle drums, we grab our bikes and converge from every corner of our side of town at the same time. A congregation of believers at the altar of broad-spectrum pesticide. We charge into the fabulous veil of DDT mist, pedalling full blast to make sure to be completely enveloped in the cloud. If you squint, you can see the reflectors on the back of our banana seats and the tops of our monkey bars. It is the highlight of the summer. Better than a soft swirl of quasi-dairy product dipped in butterscotch. The type of dairy product that's one part air and two parts chemicals. Nobody's parents pay the least bit of attention to our DDT adventures. They're making dinner or mowing the lawn or reading the paper or rolling cigarettes. "You kids better put your bikes away properly. I'm not going looking for them," Dad says.

Then there are the black flies. In addition to a monsoon's worth of standing water, we have an abundance of creeks and streams and waterfalls. Really, really cold creeks, streams and waterfalls. We wait all winter for the magic day when the last crust of snow in the shadow of the street lamps evaporates into a pouf of salted road sand so we can reclaim the outdoors without risk of frostbite. And that's the day when peak runoff gets smacked in its face with the first swarm of black flies.

Black flies are pretty much the Yin to mosquitos' Yang. Mosquitos like it hot. Black flies like it cold. Mosquitos sting. Black flies bite. Mosquitos help their dinner along by injecting an anticoagulant, causing an allergic reaction. Or in my case, creating welts the size of golf balls that last well past Labour Day. Black flies just chomp off a hunk of flesh and let the blood do its thing. Natural coagulation is more "natural," after all. You have to give them that. Together, mosquitos and black flies create a sacred, universal whole of horribleness. Complementary. Interconnected. Evil incarnate.

The 1960s method of black fly self-defence is nylon stockings. Our mothers figure this out even without the internet. Any stocking with a life-threatening run is sliced off at mid-thigh, tied in a knot on the cut end, and voila, black fly kryptonite for kids. The stocking cap protects your forehead, ears and upper neck from bites. It does nothing for your eyes. Instead, once the black flies realize that ears are off the menu, they switch tactics to eyelids and tear ducts. Hordes of children wearing stocking caps with blood dripping down our eyelids roam the streets like bald zombies, in search of semi-bugless summer fun. Nobody thinks this is strange.

2

Living Better Atomically

It was all Winston Churchill's fault. He decided the British Commonwealth needed a foothold in the U.S. Manhattan project, and depending on how you look at it, Canada drew the short or long straw. And the chosen site for nuclear excellence was Chalk River, Ontario.

The designated location was not the result of a random pointing of Churchill's finger on a map full of nothingness. It was a perfect and perfectly deliberate choice. There's lots of water from the Ottawa River, because apparently water plays some sort of role in making atoms do their nuclear thing. An army base nearby in Petawawa had a handy supply of German prisoners of war to deploy on manual labour projects, although in 1944 they didn't know there would be a hard stop in a year. The parcel of land that formed the site for the town and the nuclear plant sits smack dab in the middle of nowhere, but of course it was not undiscovered. It was a traditional camping ground for the Algonquin peoples, who were probably told they had plenty of other places to camp, like Algonquin Park, for example. The Indigenous landlords also offered up the name of the company town, Deep River, as their legend told of a bottomless section of the Ottawa

River just off shore. Nobody seemed concerned the Germans will be shipped back eventually if all goes well with the war thing and they'll all know what's going on up in the wilds of Canada, but quite probably the lack of concern was because no one would be able to find the place. Because nobody would be smart enough to think civilization could be forged from bush this dense, as unlikely as Machu Picchu materializing from the jungles of Peru.

A phalanx of physicists from the U.K. and Canada descended on the brand-new research outpost. About fifty of them. I can imagine them, happy to begin smashing particles and presiding over invisible science, round spectacles polished, lab coats neatly pressed and hair flying about with a permanent static charge.

The first job was to get a reactor or two up and running to start the research that will contribute to bombs and nuclear weaponry. This is called "going critical" in nuclear lingo and it all went swimmingly. So well, in fact, that it caught the attention of Russia, which was very interested in gaining a shortcut to their desired destination of nuclear dominance.

By 1952, both the nuclear research facility and the company town were under the wing of the brand-new Atomic Energy of Canada Limited. AECL was founded with a mandate to promote peaceful uses for atomic energy. A force for good, not evil. Unfortunately, especially today, not everyone has the same definition of good. Or evil. Depending on which side of the fence you occupy, nuclear power is either the most sensible way to deal with the ravages of fossil fuel consumption or likely to end civilization as we know it. The jury is still out.

But both good and evil are having rather a heyday in the mid-twentieth century.

The 1950s and '60s were a fantastic time to be a housewife, a milkman, a car manufacturer, a physicist, a rocket scientist or a spy. It was the zenith of the golden age of atomic science and espionage.

* * *

The 1960s are all about the future. Probably because of the technological advances spearheaded by the space race, there's an inordinate amount of time spent imagining what life will offer us in the new millennium. All of us kids calculate how old we will be in the year 2000. Horrifyingly ancient ages like thirty-nine and forty. Older than our mothers.

A utopian future awaits us. *Popular Science* magazine is quite certain that houses will be mostly self-maintaining and that anything the house can't do itself will be handled by the household robot. Our post-millennium work week is going to max out at twenty hours because computers will do all the work and our offices will be bereft of paper. We all know how well that worked out.

Another grand pronouncement: by 1980, twenty-five percent of all money spent on apparel will be for paper clothes. This was predicted in 1966 when the paper dress was invented. I never had a paper dress because the "one size fits all" wasn't my size. It wasn't paper like the kind of paper you write on, but more like the texture of a J Cloth, with your choice of two psychedelic patterns: the blue and green one or the red and pink one. Soon, we will wear our paper finery while going out on the town in our flying cars.

You might think the space race, the cold war and the birth of nuclear power happily coexisted in the same era but had nothing to do with each other. In fact, they were symbiotic. When the Russians launched the Sputnik satellite in 1957, four months before the U.S. managed to get one off the ground, it was a direct shot across the bow of North America into the flank of the Pentagon. It was a flick of the middle finger in the general direction of U.S. superiority in all things and also sent the memo that the Soviet Union was capable of deploying intercontinental nuclear weapons. This amped up the space race and in particular, the race to get to the moon. We were enthralled with the space thing and apprehensive about the nuclear annihilation thing but didn't connect the dots that we couldn't have the excitement of the former without the threat of the latter.

I was one of at least 600 million people watching the live broadcast of Neil Armstrong walking on the moon in July 1969. It was on my brother's birthday, even better than cake. I remember the TV event being at night just before bedtime. In reality, it was at 8:17 p.m. GMT, or 4:17 p.m. EDT. Maybe it seemed like later because we were all inside, glued to the television on a perfectly good sunny day. The picture was so grainy and jerky it was hard to see exactly what was going on, which will later prove to be ideal corroboration for the whole thing being fake. Neil did his thing, leaving out the crucial "a" in his "one small step for man, one giant leap for mankind" speech, and I think there was a set of golf clubs and several biodegradable golf balls (do things degrade on the moon?) involved. But the notion that Earth people could float around in outer space and live to tell the tale was truly the only appropriate use for the word "fantastic." At least in 1969.

* * *

Inexplicably, Tang still exists. There are currently more than thirty flavours of Tang, which is quite disconcerting. They are welcome to keep trying, but I can't believe that even one of a thousand flavours would actually taste good. The brand name comes from "tangerine," which is an optimistic approximation of the original flavour. Tang came on the market in 1959 but it really took off, so to speak, when it became the beverage of choice on the Gemini space missions starting in 1962. This doomed us all to several years of Tang, Tang and more Tang. There was an obsessive fascination with powdered food in the 1960s. Maybe because we were all getting prepared to live on the moon, or perhaps on Mars if the moon turns out to be too polluted with golf balls. There was always a plastic jug of Tang in our fridge, the liquid a colour of orange not found in nature. Even after it's mixed with water, it has a shelf life of forever plus two years. Even though every glass contains an entire week's dietary allotment of sugar, a space age metallic taste prevails. I think we only ever had one jug of Tang, which lasted about five years before going down the sink to live in perpetuity in the sewer.

But as it turns out, Tang is actually quite a versatile product. The story is that when dishwashers became an aspirational kitchen appliance in the late 1960s, creative housewives discovered Tang was a stealth dishwasher detergent. I'm guessing either Tang was much cheaper than dishwasher powder or the kids all went on a Tang strike and the mothers needed to do something to use up their Tang stockpile. Kraft sternly failed to condone the off-label use for the product, although the company did concede the citric acid lurking within the orange powder was an effective cleaning agent. If only the dinner plates didn't come out with a rusty tinge.

Tang is also subversive because it's part of the reason we aren't allowed to bring liquids onto planes. It was a component of the liquid explosive intended for use in the 2006 London transatlantic airline terrorism plot, along with hydrogen peroxide and Hexamine, which undoubtedly improved the taste.

* * *

Two spies (that I know of) lurked around early Canadian nuclear research. Bruno Pontecorvo was an Italian physicist, but not just any plain old Italian physicist. Signor Pontecorvo studied under Enrico Fermi, the guy who discovered nuclear fission. In other words, his resume was pretty solid, which is how he ended up at Chalk River in 1946. Nobody thought to ask him about his political views and Facebook didn't exist, so the fact he was a card-carrying member of the French Communist Party stayed under the radar for a while. Maybe they just checked with the Italian Communist Party, who had never heard of him, and called it a day.

Pontecorvo's specialty was muons and neutrinos, and that's about all I can tell you about that, except that muons are like electrons only they have more mass and they turn into neutrinos when they decay. You can see how this would keep a physicist minding his own business and staying out of trouble for some time, until he decided to defect to Russia in 1950 to continue mucking about with neutrinos. The chronology gets a little hazy after that since it's filtered through the Iron Curtain. But we do know he was in the control room when the Chalk River NRX reactor came online in July 1947.

Even after the whole decamping to Russia thing, there was some doubt that Bruno (if I can presume to be so familiar) was really a spy, but I think I have the definitive proof that he was, or at least that he definitively exhibited spy behaviour. Sometime in the late 1940s, while he was still hanging around Deep River, Bruno was anointed with the nickname "Ramon Novarro." Novarro was a famous actor who began his movie career in silent films, where he was a big hit in movies like *Ben-Hur* because of his skimpy clothes. His star power really took off when he inherited the official title of "Latin Lover" after Rudolph Valentino died. It turns out Novarro got murdered in Los Angeles in 1968, but I'm pretty sure this had nothing to do with Bruno. Anyhow, Bruno's quintessential Novarro moment was when he travelled from Deep River to Boston for some R&R with two women, neither of whom was his wife. I picture cigarette holders, martinis and fast cars, although I can't quite reconcile this scenario with Boston, where high fashion consisted of high-quality gumboots in 1947. The fact remains, though, that the blueprints for the NRX reactor and some Chalk River uranium turned up in the Soviet Union after Bruno's defection and the other spy, Alan Nunn May, denied any involvement. And who doesn't believe a spy?

There is no dispute about the spyness of Mr. Nunn May because he pleaded guilty to Russian espionage for nuclear secrets in 1946. He was a British physicist and lifelong member of the Communist Party, a fact that also failed to surface when he was recruited as part of the U.K. contingent at Chalk River. Not only that, Nunn May and Pontecorvo were tasked with picking the brains of Manhattan Project scientists when they visited Canada, in essence making them double agents: spying for Britain and Russia. Where's James Bond when you need him?

But I know none of this. My dad goes to work and comes home and plays golf in the summer and curls in the winter. The atoms at the plant silently careen off the walls and spew out mutant particles: molybdenum-99, iridium-192, deuterium, tritium, protium. And they mostly keep to themselves. Just like the dinosaurs in Jurassic Park.

3

A Man, a Plan, a Town

The impeccably planned town of Deep River was designed by a guy named John Bland. I did not make up his name. If you are an aficionado of architecture you will probably know Mr. Bland. If you aren't, let me fill you in. Apparently, he was a big deal at McGill University in Montreal where he bootstrapped the school of architecture into something of a "thing." Eventually, he hooked up with two guys named Vincent Rother and Charles Elliot Trudeau, the latter of whom may ring a bell because of his brother Pierre. Both from a family of overachievers with poor imagination when it comes to middle names.

The firm of Rother, Bland and Trudeau threw its hat in the ring but did not win the job of building Toronto's new city hall. However, they did design the Labyrinth pavilion at Expo 67. My dictionary says a labyrinth is a structure with "intricate passage ways and blind alleys." Which kind of explains a lot about how things ended up in our town.

Planned urban enclaves have been around as long as the Julian calendar. Apparently, Mr. Caesar specialized in gathering up a few hundred people and sequestering them wherever he decided the Empire ought to be that it wasn't.

Much later, medieval European fancy folk used to create villages in their own image to compete with each other for prestige and of course money. There have been many planned places since then, with varying degrees of success. For example, the town of Celebration, in Osceola, Florida, was manufactured out of a swamp in 1994 by the Walt Disney Company as an imagining of the perfect American suburb. The great fanfare that accompanied Celebration's creation did not persist, because living in Disneyland turns out to be kind of creepy. And also, maybe because any time you venture outside of your fake Victorian house you have to listen to a music soundtrack on two-hour repeat pumped out of fake rocks.

Master-planned communities are revered by their proponents as perfect antidotes for urban sprawl. Since Deep River's potential sprawl is already neatly cordoned off by the river, the highway and the impenetrable bush, the potential for reverting to wilderness is much more a possibility than the development of big box plazas and chain restaurants, although my teenage self would not have complained about any of that.

* * *

Prior to his later architectural triumphs, Mr. Bland sat down with his No. 2 graphite pencil and set to work creating our terrarium. He sketched a crescent here, a winding trail there, and every so often punctuated it with cul-de-sacs. The first commandment of suburban planning is to have a few straight roads to funnel the through-traffic in and out, then hang them with a necklace of narrow streets like tributaries of the Amazon, bending every way it is possible to bend, to keep local traffic local. This may work well in an actual suburb where there is such a thing as through traffic. In our case, traffic is not traffic unless it is local. Even after they did away with the guardhouse, anyone accidently venturing off Highway 17 into town is spotted and dealt with within one block by several keen eyes wondering why there is a strange car on Deep River Road.

The shopping district in the centre forms a town quadrilateral rather than a town square, a daringly rakish sweep of the pencil by Mr. Bland. The shopping options are actually not all that shameful: banks, grocery stores, boutiques and a miniature Eaton's department store with everything from high fashion to fine china to lawnmowers. No need to ever leave even if there was somewhere else to go. The checkout clerk at the grocery store (who probably lives next door) reminds you to buy the birthday candles and extra milk for the party. The proprietor of the clothing store sells you the skirt that goes with the sweater you bought last week. The same sweater everyone else has, in blue, pink or green. The stores close on Sunday and half a day mid-week. The movie theatre swaps double features every Wednesday and Saturday. The steam plant whistle blows every day at 4:30 to remind us it's 4:30. The rhythm of the day and week never changes. Everything goes according to plan.

* * *

Thanks to Mr. Bland, it is impossible to get from A to B without detouring through G, M and W. However, he did make sure to scatter parks, wild spots and schools throughout the town so you don't need to bother going outside of your own neighbourhood for recreation or education. So we don't. The shopping centre in the middle of town is an invisible force field that stops my local cohort dead in its tracks. Until we are thrown together in grade 7, kids from the east side rarely intersect with kids from the west side. I have no idea what goes on past the middle of town but that doesn't bother me. My flat earth is complete as it is. No need to mess with dragons yet.

On my side of town, everyone's parents seem to know who I belong to even if I have never heard of them. I am sauntering home from downtown with a new *Archie* comic when someone's mother slows her woody station wagon, rolls down the window and asks me if I want a ride home. "I don't know who you are," I say, being well schooled in the requisite rules of stranger danger that are about as useful to me as learning how to calculate pi to the fifteenth decimal using a slide rule (and of course, spoiler alert, eventually I am required to do exactly that).

"Don't worry, Susie, I know your mother and who you are," she replies. Except for the Susie part, this seems like a reasonable response. But I'm in a hurry to get home to crack open the *Archie* and find out whether or not Veronica is on the ins or outs, so I hop in the car. She revs up the engine and drives around and about the snakes-and-ladders streets before dropping me off outside a beige bungalow that's nowhere near my blue one. I still don't know who she was or who she thought I was. But any brush with pseudo-anonymity, however fleeting, is to be savoured. Like a good Jughead storyline.

* * *

The original houses that populated Mr. Bland's avenues and cul-de-sacs were rounded up and transported in their entirety from various army bases that didn't need them after the war. I imagine a house-wrangler herding them onto the backs of trucks then setting off in a convoy of Monopoly pieces, the houses apprehensively waiting to find out whether they will land on Boardwalk or be stuck on Baltic Avenue.

The first war-time fours and sixes were plopped down fully formed. An instant town. Like instant coffee with powdered milk, much better than the real thing. A "four" has four rooms including the kitchen. A "six" has six rooms with the addition of two slanted-ceiling bedrooms upstairs and an encroachment of real estate on the main floor courtesy of the stairs. The fours and sixes huddle around the middle of town like settlers circling the wagons. As Mr. Bland's streets, roads and avenues flow outward, the domestic architecture branches out as well. There are square, two-story singles and semis clad in grey asbestos siding bungalows on concrete pads, and the exotic mid-century modern "brown houses" with vaulted ceilings, which back onto the "wood paths," winding walkways from nowhere to nowhere. The streets are named after both halves of our existence: scientists and trees. Darwin, Newton, Rutherford, Fermi and Kelvin. Birch, maple, spruce, alder and poplar. There's always a constant reminder of the world we inhabit, most certainly all part of Mr. Bland's grand scheme if not his grand plot.

Our town is planned within an inch of its life. There's nothing for anyone to decide. Everything has already been decided, including the colours of the houses. Inside and out. On my side of town, no blue house is ever beside another blue house. The green houses are beside the yellow houses. And if you draw the short straw you get a pink house. You have to make sure to remember the colour of your house, otherwise you might barge in and sit down to someone else's dinner. The one in the beige version of your house, perhaps. And maybe the people in the beige house are serving tuna casserole while back in your blue house twin you are expected to eat roast beef and damn well like it. Frequent house colour amnesia has its advantages and is pretty easy to pull off when you're six years old. I wish I had figured that out.

The neighbourhood is a permeable membrane. Our houses are interchangeable. Each fridge contains the same Kool-Aid and bologna. I remember each mother feeding whichever kids show up at lunchtime. If your own kids don't show up, they must be somewhere else getting fed and they'll probably materialize at dinner time. Or not. We are as undifferentiated as plankton.

* * *

You might think asbestos is a bad thing. In the 1960s, you would be wrong. That's because asbestos is a master of disguising its carcinogens as durable, colourful flooring that's ideal for high traffic areas like schools, hospitals and prisons. Pretty much anywhere you can collect lots of people to maximize exposure to noxious substances while minimizing fire hazards. And of course, it's a fantastic choice for residential aesthetics.

Our house and all the houses around us have asbestos tile on the floor. It's red in the kitchen, beige in the living room, green in the bathroom and blue in the bedrooms, just like everyone else's house. The walls are beige, just like everyone else's house. The siding is horizontal, just like everyone else's house.

Asbestos tile is twelve-by-twelve-inch rigid, flat squares, so hard it can withstand thousands of footprints without wilting. It is also a terrific raceway for metal Dinky Toys. My brother winds up the wheels on the tiny firetruck by moving it backwards on the floor, then sets it down to career across the hallway and smash into the baseboard. If you do this often enough, the tiles near the wall start to lose their cool and disintegrate around the edge. Asbestos tile might be a good choice for prisoners, but it is no match for six-year-olds.

* * *

We move to a brand spanking new house in 1966, when my father buys a vacant lot unmolested by Mr. Bland and gets our very own corner of the bush tamed into submission. Our new house is as modern as it can possibly be. There are aqua fixtures in the bathroom, sliding glass doors to the patio, and hardwood floors smothered in wall-to-wall carpet, some of it two-tone shag. This is all very exciting, especially because I can now choose the colour of my room.

My chosen colour is purple. Purple was having a moment way before Prince claimed it as his own. My vision is walls coated in dark, pulsing purple. The kind of purple that would gleam its psychedelic hue to full effect under a black light, because I'm going to do my best to acquire one to illuminate my "Maharishi with the Beatles" poster. I crave walls as far removed from my bungalow beige as possible. Unfortunately, my vision does not match my mother's and unfortunately my mother is in charge of selecting the paint chips.

What I actually get is dainty violet walls. I know violet has its own spectrum on the official colour wavelength and everything, but there's a reason why there is no band called *Deep Violet* and no song called "Violet Haze." Violet is as wimpy as a white toilet. And my bedroom walls might as well be white because you have to hold a piece of paper up to them to even see a whisper of violet. I compensate by wearing nothing but purple until I discover black. Curse you and your land of meticulously-designed and curated mediocrity, Mr. Bland. Where's Bruno Pontecorvo when you need him?

4

Dads Go to Work

Every morning at 07:42, all the dads open their front doors and walk to the corner to wait for the bus. Not all the same corner, mind you. They arrive at different corners all around town where a fleet of buses makes the rounds to ensure everyone gets picked up at precisely 07:45. I don't know what they talk about for the three leisurely minutes available for pre-ride banter. Maybe yesterday's hockey game or tomorrow's curling match. All the dads go to work together, eat lunch together, come home together, and recreate together. Kind of like a minimum-security prison or maybe an English boarding school, which, come to think of it, are pretty much the same thing. There are no secrets for very long, except of course if you happen to be a spy and only share your secrets with Russia or your most recent bed companion.

There are no lunch bags on the bus nor Thermoses of coffee because everyone's food and drink requirements are met by the plant cafeteria. At ten o'clock the morning coffee break trolley comes around with hot beverages and a full roster of tea biscuits, with raisins or without. At noon, the dads line up with their trays for tomato-with-rice soup, hot roast beef sandwiches and shimmering cubes of green Jell-O in glass dessert bowls. Lunch ends at 12:45. The buses depart at 16:20.

The plant buses are army green, with the AECL logo on the side. The AECL logo is a stylized "A" that looks like a pentagram without the line that connects the right-hand point with the bottom left. The horizontal line ends with a solid circle that's supposed to represent an atom in mid-whiz. It's kind of lame. The part above the windshield of the bus that shows the destination says CRNL, just in case anyone getting on the bus isn't quite sure where they work. There is only one destination and only one stop. The bus convoy turtles its way along the highway for six miles, then turns left onto the plant road to head down to the guard gate, discharges its passengers, picks up the people from the previous shift and then turns around to make the reverse trip.

All I know is my dad goes out of the house every morning and gets on a bus, and gets off a bus at the end of the day. I'm not in school yet or if I am in school it's kindergarten and only a half day. My little brother bears the brunt of my whims between breakfast and dinner. We play "dads go to work." This involves me pretending to be my dad on the bus, while my brother plays the dual role of both the bus and the bus driver. I grab him at the waist and propel him forward, shuffling my feet at his heels to move us around the living room in a circle. This lasts for about one-and-a-half circuits before my brother stages a three-year-old sit-in and refuses to stand up, sending the pretend bus into the pretend ditch. I am convinced that what my dad does is ride the bus all day. Where the bus goes and what he does while riding the bus is not information I'm particularly interested in.

Mothers don't get on the bus. Except for Cathy's mother, which is kind of weird. I don't know why she would be needed on the bus. Maybe she makes the lunches because that's what mothers do when they aren't putting new wax on the asbestos floor tiles or taking old wax off the asbestos floor tiles. Mothers spend a lot of time making meals, which in my house is a particularly thankless job. My mother makes us eat porridge for breakfast in the fall and winter. Cream of wheat with gelatinous white lumps. Oatmeal with gelatinous beige lumps. Red River cereal that hides hateful brown seeds in its gelatinous brown lumps. On the other hand, brown sugar is involved so it's not a complete fail. Lunch is usually good, though, because I can pick the kind of sandwich I want. Cheese, please. Or peanut butter in a pinch. Tomato soup is fine, but minestrone is just gross. And another thing that's just gross is dinner. I don't like peas. I don't like spaghetti sauce. I don't like roast beef. I don't like gravy. I don't like sauce in general. And maybe I don't like eating in particular. This is a constant source of angst for my mother's not-so-inner dietician. "You don't eat enough to keep a bird alive," she says. Every. Single. Meal.

The good thing about mothers is they play bridge. The card tables get set up in the living room about an hour before the bridge ladies descend. My mother spreads out the white tablecloths and gets out the iron to fix the creases so the table surface is as smooth as a baby's bum. I am not quite sure why the iron doesn't melt the plastic top of the card table, but maybe I am not as proficient in science as she is. She adjusts the sides of the cloth to make them equally parallel to the floor, uses a ruler to make sure they are all the same length from the floor, then goes back to the kitchen to put the coffee on. The minute I hear the percolator sputtering, I coerce my little brother into sneaking under the card table. "Come on," I say, "let's play camping Barbie!" He is about as interested in anything Barbie as he is in bridge, but the tent thing has some appeal. The tablecloth is not happy with its new job as tent flap. It slithers off-centre as we squirm under the edge into our secret hideaway.

Camping Barbie is fun for me but probably not for Barbie. She gets to hang from her ponytail on the corner supports of the card table to get away from the bears that lurk outside the tent. I decide to undo Barbie's ponytail because it might be easier to tie her up that way. Barbie has a piece of hair wrapped around the base of her ponytail right near her head, which holds it in place. I use one of the butter knives set out on the bridge table to wiggle her hairband loose enough so I can take it off. That's when the error of my ways becomes apparent: Barbie has been hiding a secret. She is completely bald beneath a comb-over of massive proportion. Her hair now hangs down around the circumference of her head, making her look like a sasquatch that likes to wear high heels. Unfortunately, the removal of the ponytail wrap is not reversible and I end up with a permanent sasquatch Barbie. Just as I hear the coffee pot stop gurgling, we scramble out of the tent. I straighten the tablecloth as best as a six-year-old can and drag my brother over to the couch where I pretend to read him Dr. Seuss. "One fish, two fish," I recite by rote.

My mother comes briskly out of the kitchen, heels denting the asbestos tile. She yells, "What happened to that tablecloth?!"

I look up from Dr. Seuss with wide-eyed dismay. How could there be a problem with the tablecloth? Nobody here except us kids reading about red fish and blue fish. "I don't know," I say. "Barbie was playing under there, though." The doorbell rings. It's Mrs. Ross and Mrs. Joyce. Saved by the bell. I hope Barbie doesn't get in trouble.

Bridge involves the silver tea pot, the silver sugar dish, and more importantly, the silver sugar cube picker-upper. The sugar cube picker-upper proudly has only one purpose in life: to transport the sugar cube to the teacup because spoons and loose sugar are so déclassé. Or maybe because the sugar cube picker-upper was on the wedding registry at Birks and someone bought it because it was the cheapest thing on the silverware list and it would be wasteful not to use it. Regardless, the sugar cube picker-upper is alone in thinking it only has one purpose in life.

My big brother likes bridge day so he can give it another job: lunar landing module.

The sugar cube picker-upper is a slim, cylindrical tool about the circumference of a stick-pen and four inches long, with a metal plunger on the top. When you press the plunger down, four arms open up on the south end, like a claw, to grab the sugar cube. My brother moves into action as a lunar landing expert. "Houston, module approaching moon surface. All systems go." He says with great authority. He lifts the device about an arm's length above the card table and prepares for the delicate descent to the moon. From my angle, it appears it will be a crash landing, because his hand comes down in one fell swoop at about the speed of sound. At the last minute he presses the plunger and deploys the arms. Almost in time. But it turns out sterling silver is kind of soft and the arms bend inward. Oh-oh. Houston, we have a problem. We quickly hide the mortally wounded sugar picker-upper in my Barbie suitcase, which is always at the ready, and start playing a decoy game of Snakes and Ladders.

I think Barbie took that secret to her grave because the mystery of the missing sugar picker-upper has never been solved.

Bridge day also has another irresistible feature: party sandwiches. The best thing in the world other than eating party sandwiches is hanging around in the kitchen while they are being made. My mother gets loaves of square white bread from the bakery, cut lengthwise for pinwheels and crosswise for triple-decker fingers. The pinwheels are pink pimento cream cheese spirals coiled around a gherkin. Gherkins only get used for party sandwiches. Otherwise they are pickle *non gratae*. For kids' parties, they frequently feature peanut butter corralling a banana. I hate bananas so much I spit them out as a baby. Adult party sandwiches are just fine with me. The finger sandwiches are two layers of egg salad, tuna salad, ham salad or shrimp salad. They are definitely a salad thing. Crusts are not allowed in party sandwich territory. The proper dietician-approved technique is to spread the filling on the bread then cut off the crusts. I love these crusts with vestiges of filling on the edges. "Too wasteful to throw them away." I can eat three loaves worth of crusts without barfing. Surely enough to keep a bird alive.

At precisely 16:45 the green buses lumber down the street, signalling the end of the work day. Kids gather at the bus stop corners to greet the triumphant return of the dads from their long day on the bus. When my dad gets off, I swarm his knees and beg to carry his briefcase. I get one-on-one quality time for the whole minute it takes to walk from the bus to the front door. Once we're through the door and in the house, it's back to a firm division of kid and state. The buses go back to their garage for a good night's sleep before it's time to do the whole thing again tomorrow, porridge and all.

5

Blank Slates

School is a petri dish with a mandate to grow us from simple cells to complex biomass. The most modern 1960s pedagogical tools and techniques are deployed with abandon. My introduction to arithmetic features Cuisenaire rods. Cuisenaire rods sound like they should be in the business end of an Easy-Bake Oven. They are not. They are ten skinny, rectangular blocks of wood intended to make learning math fun. And maybe they do if you have the spatial awareness of an astronaut and a keen grasp on visual abstraction. The scabs on my knees and elbows prove I have none of these skills.

The white piece of wood is the smallest. Pretty much the perfect size to choke the average seven-year-old. The white pieces don't remain white for very long after they are kid-handled mercilessly, but they stay white enough to be distinguishable from the yellow pieces, which are five times the length of the white ones. If you put two yellow pieces together, they're the same length as the orange piece. The orange piece, which is the size of a mutant chopstick, is the perfect length for poking someone in the side or hitting someone on the head, a skill we all learn much more quickly than arithmetic.

Miss Biggs tells us to settle down and stop trying to poke each other's eyes out. "This is fun," she says. "See how it takes ten white rods to make one orange rod but only five red ones?" Of course I can see that. Anybody can see that. The question is why is this important, useful, or interesting? Miss Biggs doesn't supply an answer to my unasked question. The rods are supposed to have something to do with learning number theory, but one plus one in Cuisenaire-rod-land does not equal two. Instead, one white rod plus one white rod equals the length of a red rod. Kind of like an abacus that's lost its marbles. Instead of mucking about with sticks of wood, I decide to crack open my *Mr. Whiskers* reader. Miss Biggs can hardly fault me for getting a jump on *Mr. Whiskers Goes to Town*, the next installment in his exciting anthropomorphic feline adventure. Mr. Whiskers would know what to do with those rods. He'd bat them under the couch and feign innocence, the perfect Cheshire cat. Miss Biggs doesn't notice that I've changed the subject. She is too busy trying to get Brian to spit out a white rod. Miss Biggs finally decides we have had enough math fun and should now move on to art. Except for the rods the boys steal to throw at each other during recess. We never see Cuisenaire rods again.

Miss Biggs either has a bizarre sense of humour or is a little out of touch with who she is teaching. For today's art class, she asks us to draw a picture of where our fathers work. Maybe she is expecting to see drawings of butchering or baking or candlestick making or doctoring or lawyering. What she gets is twenty kids staring blankly at their sheets of brown craft paper then staring blankly at each other, trying to figure out how best to fake it in art class. Because none of us has any idea what our fathers do all day. I wonder if you're allowed to cheat in art class and if it's possible to flunk art class, and more importantly, if it's possible to flunk grade 2 art class. Eventually, inspiration strikes and the crayons start scratching. Most kids draw a potted plant. I draw a bus.

* * *

The Cold War was alive and well in the 1960s, and the Soviet Union had as big a red civilization-annihilation button as the U.S., but Deep River had the added twist of four nuclear research reactors nearby and being on the radar of several repatriated Russian spies who knew exactly how they worked. Or even worse, exactly how to make them stop working in spectacular fashion. Aside from exterior threats, there was also the possibility of a nuclear accident (or four).

In the years since the invention of nuclear power, nuclear accidents have become known enough to have their own scale, called the International Nuclear Event Scale (INES). Unlike the wimpy Saffir-Simpson Hurricane Wind Scale, which tops out at five, the INES goes all the way to seven. And our planet has actually been to the top of the INES hit parade twice. Once, courtesy of the Russian Chernobyl meltdown in 1986, and again in 2011, when an earthquake caused a series of unfortunate events at the Fukushima Daiichi Nuclear Power Plant in Japan. In contrast, the famous 1979 Three Mile Island accident in the U.S. only rated a five, although it retains its claim to fame as the catalyst for the acceleration of the anti-nuclear power movement.

The INES did not exist in the 1950s, when two accidents happened at the Chalk River plant. The first, in December 1952, resulted in a three-foot flood of radioactive water in the basement of the National Research Experiment (NRX) reactor building. As you might imagine, this caused some concern, so somebody got on the horn to the Americans, probably saying something like, "Manhattan, we have a problem." The immediate assessment was that the site should be mothballed under several miles of concrete, and everyone in the vicinity should walk briskly in the opposite direction and not look back. This was not the desired answer, so the Chalk River mucky-mucks huddled, talked amongst themselves and decided to clean it up. The folks on the other end of the phone in Los Alamos probably sighed heavily, then dispatched the cavalry to the rescue, in the form of U.S. army and navy personnel. It must have taken them some time to reach the Chalk River plant, although they did have more modern conveyances than the voyageurs. The troop planes landing at the army base in Petawawa must have looked like a WWIII invasion. Not at all alarming. In the meantime, AECL employees were pressed into service to sop up the water, each person taking a thirty-second shift, the maximum time permitted in order to limbo under the radiation exposure wire with extremities reasonably intact. When the Americans arrived, the cleanup crew included a guy called Jimmy Carter, who was in the navy at the time.

Then, in 1958, at the National Research Universal (NRU) reactor, some uranium caught fire when a fuel rod broke. Fuel rods are not supposed to break, by the way. Somebody, or several somebodies, snapped to it and used the handy-dandy uranium fire extinguisher to kill the blaze. Disaster averted. Except for the part about not being able to go back into the building for the entire month of June. Tough luck if you'd left your car keys behind.

* * *

When the steam plant whistle blows three times in the middle of a late October morning, it means we are having a safety drill. We have never done this before, but Miss Biggs seems to have everything under control. She calls us to attention. "Put your pencils down, class. It's time to play a fun game."

"Everything is fun and games for Miss Biggs," says my inside voice, but her notion of fun rarely jives with mine.

"Go and get your coats," she says. Half the kids keep on practising writing the letter "q" (one of the hardest ones), while the other half look like they have never heard the word coat, seven-year-old sense of urgency being less than finely honed.

Miss Biggs gives up and goes across the hall to the grade 3 room, where more highly evolved students are already buttoning up their brown duffle coats (Sears fall catalogue, page 42). She conscripts the grade 3 students to drag each of us to the back of the room to find our green corduroy jackets (Sears fall catalogue, page 38). A safety drill would never happen in the winter because it would take a good hour to corral us into our snow pants, find the mitts that match and figure out whose boots are whose. Nobody seemed to clue into this gaping hole in our preparations, and lucky for us neither did Russia.

"I want you to all walk home as fast as you can. No stopping to play! When you get home, you can eat lunch and then come back to school," instructs Miss Biggs.

No stopping to play? Where does the fun part come into this, I think to myself. We take off like bulls at Pamplona. Last one there is a dirty rotten egg. Little do we know, in an actual nuclear emergency, the last one there would be pretty much like the first one there: toast. Hold the eggs. We are, of course, unescorted by adults. The adults at the school are probably under the desks or in a secret bomb shelter.

Somehow, some teacher keeps track of how long it takes us to hurry home. My house is about as far as you can get from school. When I get there, my mother is hanging out the sheets on the clothesline like any other day. But then again, she's already home, so her part of the bargain is done and dusted. She calmly serves me a peanut butter and grape jelly sandwich, then my little legs carry me back to school to continue mastering the fine art of the lowercase "q."

I don't know who decided relying on primary school children to proceed swiftly and with great purpose to safety, while a mushroom cloud bloomed in the sky, was a good move. I also don't know why our houses were considered safe, especially since neither our bungalow nor the rest of the bungalows on the street had a basement. And more importantly, I have no clue why the dozens of buses that took our dads to work and back, and sat empty in a garage between shifts, weren't pressed into service to get us somewhere that might have been marginally more sensible. Maybe the objective was to make sure we could all vaporize together. One last, wholesome, nuclear family activity.

Anyhow, the reactors didn't melt down. Russia didn't push the button. A Kennedy got shot. Another Kennedy got shot. The Iron Curtain fell. Meanwhile, someone somewhere probably still has a neat log book tallying how fast little kids could get from school to home and back, while dodging nuclear fallout. It's probably in the box with the Cuisenaire rods. Either that, or it's in Russia.

* * *

Art doesn't happen every day, but some art days are definitely better than others. Finger-painting day, of course, is always good. Finger paint tastes kind of like white glue. The best part about white glue is the hardened, translucent bit around the Elmer's cap that can last as long as a piece of Double Bubble, minus the lame comic strip.

We have three finger paint colours to choose from: yellow, red and blue. Mixed together, these turn into a muddy, army green exactly the same colour as the plant's buses. So I usually just finger paint a bus. Kind of like a primary school Andy Warhol, bringing fresh nuance to my sole subject every week. Miss Biggs does not encourage this type of colour mixology nor my dogged commitment to perfecting my interpretation of the platonic form of the bus. I'm sure her finger painting teaching guide has a strict set of desired learning outcomes, like fine motor skills for writing readiness and spatial recognition skills for Cuisenaire rod readiness. She frowns and writes notes in her big red notebook. Maybe there *is* such a thing as flunking grade 2 art.

Our masterpieces hang up to dry at the back of the room until the final bell, when we roll them up to take home. I present my twentieth iteration of *Bus: A Study* to my mother. It spends about half an hour hanging on the fridge door before it is put away for "safe keeping." With the Cuisenaire rods, probably.

The very, very, very best art day is asbestos clay day. Asbestos is a wonder material in the 1960s. Not only does it cover our floors and insulate our walls, it is a mighty fine modelling material: malleable, full of texture and most of all fire proof. Ideal for making ashtrays.

Miss Biggs asks for a volunteer to pour the bag of asbestos into the bucket of water to make the clay. Either she knows something we don't or she is in on the secret that one of the most fun things about asbestos day is mixing up the clay. Everyone's hand goes up. Everyone practically stands on their chair to get the teacher's attention. "Me, Miss! Me, Miss! No fair, he did it last time!" Somehow, I end up winning this round. The paper bag of asbestos clay makes a satisfying whoosh as the contents avalanche into the pail. At least, most of it makes it into the pail. The remaining cloud of dust hovers over the teacher's desk then wafts lazily to the floor.

Next step, the yardstick. Three feet of stirring power wielded by three feet of kid. Miss Biggs stands at the back of the room with a tight smile on her face. For some reason I don't think asbestos day is as fantastic for her as it is for us. But we're all happy and struck with awe at the beauty of grey glop so I'm guessing Miss Biggs sees some sort of value proposition in a temporarily well-behaved classroom.

I line up to scoop up a wet handful of clay and bring it back to my desk. You can make anything you like as long as it is related to smoking. An ashtray or maybe a pipe-rest or lighter holder. The crafting of the ashtrays takes about an hour, as it is important to try several times to get just the right shape and maximize the asbestos exposure.

There's a painful art intermission while we wait, trying to will the musty, mineral smell of drying asbestos into submission. The hands on the clock over the blackboard go nowhere. The two times table gets repeated a bazillion times in an endless high-pitched monotone that could put an ashtray to sleep. One times two is two. Two times two is four. Three times two is six. Four times two is eight.

Then it's finally time to give our handiwork its coat of decorative paint. This is where our artistry really shines. We paint five-petalled pink flowers. We paint blue and white stripes. We paint a shining yellow sun. We paint a jaunty red potted plant. We paint an army green bus. It was probably lead paint.

6

My Country Is Winter

Our car tries to start, wheezing out a low, visceral growl —
like a bear waking up mid-hibernation, still too stuck in slow
motion to exert much of a fight, wanting to get back to his
dreams of summer blueberries. The engine block heater is
standard equipment here, a car's version of a down parka.
The cars all have electrical plugs dangling out of the front
grill, umbilical cords to feed them winter nutrients. Any car
left in the driveway freezes to the pavement and if by some
miracle the engine turns over, it lurches through the packed
snow on the street, the flat part of the tire thumping on the
last fourth of every rotation, its exhaust forming a permanent
cloud about a foot off the road. But that's okay. Once spring
gets here in seven months or so, it will surely sort things out.
If not, we have worse problems.

We walk to school year-round. Inclement weather is not
anyone's concern. It's just weather. Our walk is a mile, give
or take, and our winter wear is reasonably serious business.
Getting ready to leave the house for school in the winter
takes about an hour, not including the battle over eating the
porridge. First, the snow pants. Snow pants are the lower
half of a snowsuit. I am already eight, so snowsuits are a

distant unpleasant memory of having to anticipate needing to pee at least half an hour before the urgency presents itself. I have a red Stewart tartan jumper with patch pockets on the front that I wear over a red turtleneck. The lines of the plaid almost match at the side seams. The reds would pretty much be the same if my sweater tended less to the orange side of the colour wheel. My red knit stockings nicely split the colour discrepancy. Unfortunately, snow pants are not made for skirts, but skirts it is because it will be another six years before girls are allowed to not show our legs at school.

Stuffing a jumper into a pair of snow pants takes patience and skill. If I roll my skirt up past my waist, there will be a logistical problem getting my coat on and more importantly, an exposure problem when it comes to taking my pants off at the other end. So I cram as much fabric as I can down each pant leg in a Michelin Man maneuver, pull the snow pant suspenders up over my shoulders, and hope for the best. Getting the coat on is pretty straightforward, but the scarf has its challenges. I need to wind it around my neck a few times once my hood is pulled up and position it strategically to cover most of my face without obscuring my vision too much. The other problem is there is no grandmother in the world who can knit mitts that will not freeze your thumbs. Or at least no grandmother in my world.

My boots are the same as everyone else's in grade 3, boy or girl: brown rubber galoshes that go over my shoes, with an insulation value of approximately zero and slick rubber soles that skitter over the ice. There's a strap with a buckle attached near the top of the boot that's supposed to hold it on. All the kids on my street head out in a pack in winter morning twilight to trudge our way to school. There's a certain kind of squeak the snow makes under our boots when frozen rubber meets snow nearing absolute zero. Every time I pick up my foot, my boot lags about a minute behind my shoe, turning every step into two steps.

Carol and I meander and dawdle even though I can't feel my face behind a scarf that's stiff with frozen exhalation. *Where there are no sidewalks, walk facing the traffic,* Elmer the Safety Elephant says. What does he know? He's from Africa, for Pete's sake. Anyway, there's no traffic. Just pods of winter wear inhabited by kids, streaming schoolward. My snow pants make a zip-zip noise as the legs rub together. Carol and I walk in the treads left by the cars so we don't get snow coming in the top of our boots. When snow gets in your boots it gets into your shoes. And when it gets into your shoes, once you get to school it melts about mid-morning and your feet will still be wet on the trip home. The boys, though, prefer to see how deep they can go into the snowbanks. "I'm king of the castle," David says, as he jumps onto the top of the four-foot mound of snow by the curb. He sinks up to his knees, and when he lifts his feet out his boots and shoes stay behind. "Wait up, you guys! I have to find my boots!"

This is not my problem and I hate being late for school, so I scurry ahead. My fingers and toes are tingling. The first sign of frostbite.

* * *

The classroom smells like wet wool and melting snot. Thirty pairs of identical boots arrive in the hallway each morning. Miss Nelson is obsessed with ensuring our boots arrive and leave on the same pair of feet, even though nobody would ever know the difference. Her first strategy is to write our last names on the buckle strap with a black Magic Marker. Only

Miss Nelson is allowed to use the Magic Marker, after the incident with the indelible mustaches. She clearly has no sense of whimsy. This attempt at boot names works about as long as it takes us to get halfway home. The next day, thirty pairs of identical boots with identical black smudges on their straps line the hall outside the classroom.

But Miss Nelson is determined. She is always determined. I call her no-fun Nelson because of her rule that we cannot start reading lessons until everyone in the class can make it through the seven times table without mucking up seven times nine. That and because of the whole mustache thing. It really wasn't my fault. She is clearly a control freak. However, Miss Nelson is smarter than I think. Her next attempt at boot control almost hits the jackpot.

"Class," she says, "pay attention. Brian! Put that down! I have a clothespin for each of you in this box. Please pass it along to your neighbour. Brian! Clothespins do not belong on our noses! Go to the back of the room and write out the seven times table ten times!" At this point, I'm a little confused about what the clothespin is for if not for our noses. But I'm not going to risk asking Miss Nelson. The seven times table is not my friend.

"Quiet, everyone, and listen to me. Print your first name on your clothespin. What's that Ellen? Okay, if you have the same name as someone else, add the first initial of your last name. What's that Ellen? Okay then, use the first two letters of your last name. What's that Ellen? Well, just write it smaller. Ellen, you are getting dangerously close to reciting the seven times table." Miss Nelson is a little testy. "Now class, once you are done writing on your clothespin, go out in the hall and use the clothespin to attach your boots together," she instructs.

Hmmmm. Which ones are my boots? I choose a pair and claim them with my clothespin. Hopefully, this pair doesn't have buckles that freeze. Only about six months, twenty days, nine hours and thirty-two minutes of winter left to go.

* * *

What do primary school kids talk about when they slog through the snow to school in the winter, uphill both ways? Carol and I talk about our pets. Or wished-for pets. Or the tedium of pet duty. I have two turtles who live in a glass bowl with a bunch of rocks and some water. I call them Timothy and Tomothy. I don't care what anyone else calls them. T&T probably have salmonella, my mother says. She is less than enthusiastic about harbouring slimy animals and I have no idea how we ended up with them. The turtles probably have no idea either.

My job is to feed them turtle food that looks like pulverized green Styrofoam. "Not too much! If you feed them too much they'll get fat!" A fat turtle would clearly be a problem, given the shell and all, but the other problem with feeding them too much is the water in the bowl turns into green sludge. I'm afraid T&T will get sick and die in the murky water, so I take it upon myself to rinse out their bowl. My eye-hand coordination is less than stellar, so on the way to the kitchen sink I drop the bowl on the floor and the broken glass takes a divot out of the tip of my left baby finger. Timothy ends up under the fridge and never comes out. Ever. Or maybe it's Tomothy that ends up under the fridge and maybe Timothy ends up under the cupboard. They are both green with red and yellow stripes on the neck so it's pretty hard to tell who is who.

My blood is almost exactly the same colour as the kitchen floor. I get out of going to church that day and get a Band-Aid instead of stiches. Not a bad bargain. That's the end of the turtle situation and for any pets in general for quite a while. "You kids need to learn how to take more responsibility," Dad says, and goes back to practicing his putting on the living room rug, coaxing a plastic golf ball into a metal contraption that's supposed to be a hole. "Darn. Almost got that one!"

My mother says T&T have gone to turtle heaven, but we can't bury them because it's winter. "They have to go down the toilet," my mother says. "I'm not having them hang around until spring, smelling to high heaven. If they go down the toilet, they'll float out to sea where they came from." Sounds reasonable to me.

Carol and I also talk about the Beatles. In particular, which one we are going to marry. It doesn't matter if any of them are already married. We especially talk about the Beatles when playing indoors in Wenda's rec room with our Barbies, while snow squalls rage outside. The Barbies are idle props resting in our laps while wearing their best fancy shoeless Barbie outfit. No Barbie in history ever had two shoes once liberated from her box. My Barbie usually just chooses to wear the black and white bathing suit she arrived in. Whatever the season. Even today, when Fahrenheit meets Celsius at forty below zero, Barbie clings to her swimsuit model lifestyle. Maybe because that means no shoes are indicated or required. There is always a big argument over who gets dibs on Paul and who is going to be stuck with Ringo (again). Only one Beatle per person. As a testament to the wholesome influence of Barbie, we never discuss which one of the Rolling Stones we are going to run away with.

Little do we know, that over time and the attrition of George and John, Ringo morphs into a "good looking" Beatle. Similarly, in the twenty-first century, Keith Richards is on both the best dressed list and the zillionaire list. If only we'd known, our choices would have been better.

* * *

Winter is fun, or so I am told. I don't like the cold. I don't like to go down hills. And more importantly, I don't like to go down hills fast. All things that winter "fun" seems to entail. However, it's either get with the program or sit inside by myself reading. I think reading is a much better idea. My mother doesn't think so. She's busy polishing the wax on the asbestos tile in the kitchen with the electric polisher that hovers over the floor like a robot. She yells at me over the whine of the motor. "Why did we bother getting you that toboggan? Got out and play. I don't want to see anyone back here until dinner time. And don't walk on the floor! It's not dry yet."

No one has ever seen a rabbit at Rabbit Rock, but that's what it's called. Rabbit Rock is a granite protrusion across from my house, surrounded by red pine trees and sumac bushes and blueberry patches. It has at least a two-percent grade and is roughly three toboggan lengths long, but it's the best hill we have without involving station wagons and adult participation. We don't want to encourage adult participation because it usually doesn't end well. Like, for example, when a critical mass of kids is crying because they've fallen off the toboggan face first in crusty snow or crashed into a snowbank, they make us all go home.

My wooden toboggan weighs about twenty pounds naked. It has a loose, green vinyl, padded cushion, whose only apparent purpose in life is to become coated with ice and freeze solid, adding another five pounds to the situation. Since the toboggan is a three-seater (with an optional fourth if someone has brought along a younger sibling), it has handy raised cross-pieces to mark out the individual rear-end territory. All the better to bruise your tailbone. I haul the dead weight up the snow-packed rock and get into the driver's seat. Sara and Jane pile on the back and we sit there, not moving. My passengers quickly tire of going nowhere and get off the toboggan to execute self-propelled sideways rolls down the hill. It's faster than the toboggan and is a much better way to completely encrust your jacket with snow.

I now have full custody of the toboggan. Somehow, because it's all mine, I forget I hate tobogganing. Time to experiment. What will happen if I stand up on the toboggan? I position my feet between the first and second raised slats and grab the rope like I'm getting ready to ride a rodeo bull. The toboggan doesn't move. *Objects at rest tend to stay at rest*, Mr. Newton reminds me.

I use my right foot to push the sled forward and shift my boot back quickly as I start moving downhill. I feel as elegant as the lady who comes around the mountain driving six white horses. "And they'll all come 'round to meet her when she comes," I sing with my inside voice. My boots slide back and forth as the toboggan starts to roll forward. I hit the steepest part of Rabbit Rock and suddenly I'm really moving, gliding over the crust on the snow like I'm waterskiing. And by some miracle, I'm still upright. If I had long hair it would be streaming out behind me, echoing the plume of snow being kicked up by the curve at the front of the toboggan. If this was an Olympic sport I would be on the top of the podium for sure.

An object continues to move at a constant velocity unless acted upon by a force, Mr. Newton intones. That's when the five-foot high snow bank intersects with the sled and interrupts my flawless run. The wood stops dead and jounces with the impact. I fall sideways, luckily with enough padding in my snow pants to bruise only my delusions of grandeur. I guess I'll stick to skating, which only involves being out in the cold and going fast sideways. Probably a better chance at the podium that way anyhow. Or at least an equal chance.

Then David shows up with a flying saucer: a concave piece of round aluminum. He puts it down at the top of the rock, backs up to take a run for it and jumps on top. David spins down the slope, handily sails over the snowbank, crosses the road and lands upside down in the ditch. What idiot ever thought wood, rectangular and flat was a good aerodynamic choice? Aluminum, round and convex is clearly the way to go. The space age wins another round.

By the end of the afternoon, the edge of the saucer is ringed with wool mitts stuck to the metal by balls of snow. It's pretty clear that Santa is going to have to corner the market on flying saucers this Christmas. Or maybe not. I'll be nine by then and surely too old for this. Please, please tell me I'll be too old for this.

7

We Don't Need No Stinking Playground

"Do you kids need a lunch?" my mother asks, as I start to run out the door on the morning of an average summer day. My mother is always all about eating meals at the proper time but in this instance, it is not a bad idea. I wait with nine-year-old patience while she slaps some ham on white sandwich bread, spreads a good swath of yellow mustard, positions some iceberg lettuce, cuts it into four squares and encases it in wax paper. I hate apples but she throws one in the paper bag anyway. The cookies aren't even store-boughten. Why can't we ever have store-boughten? I don't ever take anything to drink. Certainly not bottled water, which has the good sense to not yet exist. We drink directly from the creeks and the river, cupping our hands to spoon the water into our mouths and throwing every second handful towards whoever is in water-shot. Beaver fever and any other freshwater parasite perils do not exist either. At least not to us.

Hikes are what kids do in the summer hours after breakfast and before swimming lessons. Hikes mean crashing about in the bush discovering things, both benign and malignant. Right where my house sits, the street screeches to a halt and evaporates into the bush. The end of my street is also the end of town. The end of town is also the end of human intervention on the wilderness. So the gateway to unfettered fun is right out my back door. "Here, take this with you and pick some blueberries while you're at it," my mother says, as she shoves an empty sour cream container in my direction.

I hate picking blueberries and conveniently forget to take the container with me. "Gotta go. Everyone's already waiting at the path."

Today's hike is a mission to the firebreak. If you confidently whack your way through the underbrush for ten or twelve bug bites, you reach the firebreak. The firebreak is like a path left by a stampede's worth of tyrannosaurus rex, rampaging the length of town from the edge of the golf course road all the way down to the river, leaving nothing but trampled branches and uprooted stumps. It is a clearing about thirty feet wide that's intended to prevent a forest fire from breaching the edges of the town and protect us from being vapourized by nature's evil whims, but most likely, given the general futility of reasoning with a bush fire, the wilderness gap would be about as effective as asking people to line up politely for free beer at the Legion Hall on Saturday night. Since my house is one of the first outposts of civilization it would encounter in its path, I'm guessing any forest fire worth its reputation would roar across the firebreak in a nanosecond and eat my Beatles records for lunch before heading on downtown to consume the Monkees paraphernalia at the shopping plaza for dessert.

On the way to the firebreak, we pass Fun Rock. I don't know who, but some kid with a firm grasp of literal nomenclature dubbed it that and of course it stuck. And why not? Fun Rock is the animated short in front of the main feature. Fun Rock is an eight-foot high *Flintstone*'s boulder discarded in the primeval forest by an ice age glacier. This type of rock is called an erratic, because it appears to have been dropped out of the sky into somewhere completely unlikely. Like a lemonade stand showing up in the middle of the desert. And that's kind of what it is to us.

The fifty-foot trip to the firebreak takes at least an hour as the kid flies. Frank needs to stop and tie his shoes every ten minutes. "Come on, Frank! Didn't you learn how to tie your shoes in grade 1? You're such a baby!" David says. Susan's little brother sits down on the path and starts crying because he can't keep up.

"It's not my fault! My mother made me bring him! She has to go and get her hair done and boys aren't allowed! It's not my fault! Jerry, I'm going to leave you here if you don't smarten up right now!" Susan says.

Then Frank and David start arguing about whether Batman or Superman is better. "Superman is stupid. How come nobody recognizes him when he puts glasses on? And why does he need a cape? I thought he could fly on his own. He doesn't need a cape. You only need a cape if you can't fly," argues Frank.

"You're a stupid head and Batman's a big fat faker! He can't even fly with his cape. That's why he needs the Batplane," says David.

"Come on you guys," I say. "We're almost at Fun Rock. Last one there gets to change Jerry's diaper."

We pull off the path at Fun Rock to have lunch. We usually stave off eating until at least ten o'clock. And save our cookies for at least ten thirty. Then we fling our uneaten apples off into the general direction of the ferns and blueberry bushes, extra points if it hits a birch tree and flies in twelve different directions. We know how to survive in the bush.

The woods around Fun Rock harbour several species of elusive wildflowers. We try to spot jack-in-the-pulpits, which have two-tone green stripes that meld into the forest floor and a hooded leaf that shields its flowers, allowing it to hide in plain sight. Poison ivy can fool you into thinking it's a jack-in-the-pulpit because of the three shiny leaves, so we are careful not to get too close, because of that and also the fact that jack-in-the-pulpits excrete oxalic acid, which causes kidney failure. But only if you eat it, and we're not that dumb. Lady's slippers are equally evasive and only marginally less toxic: they specialize in a chemical called cypripedin that burns your skin, probably to protect the delicate pink orchid flowers from grubby kid fingers. Trilliums won't kill you, but rumour has it if you pick one the police will show up at your door in seconds flat and charge you with murdering a provincial flower. How the police know what goes on at Fun Rock is a mystery, but we're pretty sure they know. Everyone knows everything around here.

At first glance, the firebreak doesn't look like much. If you look closely, it's just scrubby undergrowth, roots and dead branches. But if you squint, it looks like a landing strip for alien spaceships. It's a strange pause in the dense forest where anything unusual could happen. Spacemen may not land here, but they could. We walk with our eyes towards the ground and not just because of the piles of bear poop. We look down because we don't want to miss the natural treasures on the forest floor, like iridescent clam shells dropped by shore birds or perfectly forked twigs ideal for wienie roasts. Gord stops abruptly and puts his finger to his lips. The rest of us slow down and break off our discussion about last night's episode of *Bonanza*. The air is silent except for chickadee chatter and there's no musty bear smell in the wind so it must be something else. Gord bends down and picks up a flat, black rock. Only it's not a rock. It's an arrow head the size of his palm, notched around the edges and blunt on the tip. I look around as if arrows might start flying from the stand of silver and gold birch trees on the left, but no ancient archers materialize. Gord is the lucky duck today but these finds show up pretty regularly. Later in the summer, my brother finds one almost the same. Then he takes it to the first day of school for show and tell and we never see it again. Perhaps the work of a warrior ghost, repatriating it to the happy hunting ground.

The firebreak provides excellent opportunities for losing body parts, especially eyes. There's a kid who lives down the street who has a glass eye, which must be because of the firebreak. At least that's what our parents say. We go there so often our cheap canvas sneakers beat down a path through the poison ivy and other assorted dubious undergrowth. It is a secret path we share only with the several hundred kids on our side of town.

* * *

Sometimes we're lazy and go to the official playground at Cedar Park. Strangely, although there are lots of trees, there are hardly any cedars there. But there is a clearing at the edge of the park with a set of rusty monkey bars shedding lead paint, a "wheel of death" that's guaranteed to generate scabs, and a rocket ship. Not a real rocket ship, mind you. But real enough for us.

Glen says, "Dibs on the cockpit!" The pretend rocket is mounted on a forty-five-degree angle, poised for a non-NASA-compliant lift off. It's an open lattice of metal pipe shaped like a fat, hollow, sharpened pencil. It's even painted yellow, but that's probably because they used leftover fire hydrant paint. The pointy end spears a ball of metal fashioned in the same way as the body of the rocket, but it's painted red, maybe with leftover fire truck paint. I'm not quite sure what the round thing is supposed to be. Is it a pygmy planet that somehow got impaled on the rocket? Is it supposed to evoke the moon landing? Whatever the heck it is, we don't waste time dissecting its provenance. It is what it is. It's a rocket.

Glen crawls through one of the side openings and scrambles up to the top of the space craft. I pile in with Wenda and Laurie. "Let's be Apollo 1," Glen decides, which means like the astronauts on the first Apollo flight, this game will be short-lived. Glen guides us through the preflight checklist: "Booster system. Check. Guidance system. Check. Communication system. Check. Liftoff in ten, nine, eight, seven, six, five, four, three, two, ONE!" We all chant the countdown with him and make the whooshing noise that signals we're about to leave the earth. Except we don't. Just like Apollo 1. In fact, we never ever leave the earth in this rocket, which is why this playground is kind of lame. Which is why we like the firebreak.

* * *

About once a week, a bunch of us build a fort in the bush along the firebreak. If it's near the firebreak it shouldn't burn down. But our fort never lasts long enough to encounter fire danger because it has a tendency to fall apart after a few days of exposure to the elements. Either that or we forget where it is and have to start over.

"I borrowed my dad's hammer," Brian says. "I have to get it back before he finds out. And I got these nails from the can in the garage. He won't miss them. He already took them out of the old deck boards. Some of them aren't even too rusty and they're mostly pretty straight!"

We scout out the ideal spot: just off the main trail where there's three maple trees in close formation. It'll save an extra wall. There's also a good mound of twigs and branches. "You guys hold that branch up and I'll nail it in," says Brian. "It's my hammer. You guys can't use it in case you break it." Eventually, we have a triangle-shaped platform, created by cross-hatching poplar twigs between three larger branches, suspended between the maples about three feet off the ground. Brian tests it by jumping up and down. Only a few twigs break, and it looks like if you place your foot correctly, it won't fall through the cracks. Works for me.

Brian hauls the other four of us up into the open concept fort. Play time begins. Or at least play time could begin but doesn't because we're arguing about what to do. "My hammer built this fort. My fort. My rules," says Brian. "Jim, Barry and me are going to play *Hogan's Heroes*. Who wants to be Colonel Klink?"

Nina and I exchange a disgusted look. We have one of her mother's *True Confessions* magazines. We're finding out what happens when you inherit your sister's devil child and learning about the consequences of free love, and this trumps any stupid adventures any boy could possibly come up with. Nina and I abandon the fort, and in the process, dislodge the hammer, which falls down into the underbrush below us. The boys are too busy putting dibs on their favourite prisoner-of-war roles to notice either our departure or the hammer's. Brian better remember how to get back to today's version of Stalag 13 or he'll be in a whole world of butt hurt.

Forget about blueberries, the bears have picked them over anyway. There are many other berries, both advisable and unadvisable. There's wintergreen with red berries, on small shrubs with glossy Christmas-green leaves, which look appetizing but taste like what would happen if you spread Cool Mint Crest on a piece of Styrofoam. If you eat too many of them, you'll overdose on methyl salicylate, which is not recommended. No danger of that happening to me, though. I hate Cool Mint Crest. Then there are the chokecherries, a glisteningly transparent red, with a satisfying burst of juicy innards when you bite down on them, just before it becomes clear how they got their name and you struggle to spit them out before your mouth devolves into a permanent pucker. Best stick to the wild raspberries, as tiny as Thumbelina's thumb and chock full of miniature gnat-like flies that stick to my teeth. Protein.

8

Sinking Is Not an Option

Someone in Deep River, at some point, thought it was a good idea to use the natural gift of the Ottawa River to teach all the kids to swim. In a river that's a mile wide at our point of entry. In a river that beckons you gently with a great swath of pristine sand, then fails to wish you luck as it drops abruptly down to nowhere about twenty feet off shore. The depth at Oiseau Rock, just up the river near the plant, measures more than one thousand feet. Usually, except for one random day in August, the water temperature feels like it hovers just above freezing.

Choosing to wrangle with the Ottawa River is literally survival of the fittest. In the 1600s, it was prone to taking out voyageurs who thought they were just out for a pleasant pillaging, plundering canoe trip up 790 miles of water superhighway. Today, people pay good money for near-death experiences shooting the rapids in rubber dinghies, but nobody who learned to swim in the Ottawa River would ever do this. It would be too much like getting back in the tiger's cage after successfully scaling the barbed wire fence to get out.

We have an embarrassment of wide beaches paved with million-year-old silicon pulverized within an inch of its life.

The beaches all have names so you don't accidently end up at the wrong one. Only one beach is the swimming-lesson beach. Lamure Beach. If you want to know how it got that name, I have no idea. Please ask Mr. Bland.

Every afternoon, every inch of the swimming-lesson beach is infested with children, hundreds of us with a decibel level to match. Swimming lessons take place rain or shine. Because rain is just water and you're just going to get wet anyway. "Suck it up, kids. No, that wasn't thunder. Anyone leaving the water goes back down to Minnow!"

My mother and her friends usually show up at the beach around two and plant their folding lawn chairs in the shade of the pine trees at the edge of the sand. They read *Woman's Day* magazine and Arthur Hailey books and wear bathing caps covered in plastic flowers when they go in the water so they don't ruin their hair. No need to supervise kids. That's what lifeguards are for.

The beach parking lot is crammed tighter than the Tokyo subway with blue CCM gliders, pretty much the one and only kind of bike sold at the one and only hardware store. If you want to arrive and leave with the same two wheels, you have to get serious about embellishment. Girls prefer the handlebar streamer. Or maybe that's the only socially acceptable option on offer if you have two X chromosomes. The boys pilfer clothespins from the line to attach hockey cards to their back wheels. The thwack against the spokes is supposed to sound like a motorcycle. Instead, it more closely resembles the sound of a hockey card being snapped back and forth by a bike wheel.

Before and after swimming lessons there's time to hang out. My friends and I sit as far away from our mothers as possible. I amuse myself by digging cigarette butts out of the sand, but only the filtered ones. I am discerning. I don't remember why this was fun or if there was a more altruistic reason for this activity. The most likely explanation is we used the butts to bet on our euchre game. Because that's the other thing we do between swimming lessons: play euchre. Just your average, normal pastime for eight-year-olds.

By mid-afternoon, there are waves of heat rising from the sand. The loudspeaker at the lifeguard shack squawks out swimming lesson marching orders nonstop: "Minnow six to the hollow log. Tadpole eight to the base of the lifeguard tower. Bantam three to the flag pole." Four little girls sit in a circle on our towels, bums wet with sand, baby oil "suntan" lotion mixed with sweat in our hair, the soles of our feet as black as the end of a cigarette butt. It's euchre time.

I don't know who taught us euchre. Maybe someone with a sense of humour or more likely just your typical 1960s adult. Probably someone's dad. I have a teeny, tiny deck of cards about as big as my thumb. These cards are very popular with my age group, likely because no adult would ever co-opt them for a bridge game. They are also very easy to lift from Stedman's five and dime. Apparently euchre reached its popularity zenith in the nineteenth century, except for parts of Ontario with minimal opportunities for amusement, where I am told it is still hale and hearty in Legion Halls as a drinking game. Which kind of explains a lot. Euchre could drive anyone to drink.

Carol says, "I call spades as trump. I bet five cigarette butts." I check my hand and see I have the left bower. Luckily, the jack of clubs becomes a spade in these situations. Except he has to go back to being a club for the next hand. Unless someone decides to play an "ace no face" and takes three cards from the kitty. If that happens, all bets are off. Even the cigarette butt ones. You can see why we like this game. Only an eight-year-old could possibly think these rules are logical. You can probably also understand why the mere sight of a card deck causes me traumatic flashbacks to this day. Flashbacks to endless summer afternoons with endless rounds of euchre, cigarette butts piled high, with absolutely no responsibility other than to show up for swimming lessons.

Swimming lessons are serious business for everyone involved. Even little kids cannot phone it in. Attendance is taken. I'm pretty sure we are marked on a secret bell curve. I'm also pretty sure the swimming instructors huddle together between classes to blame and shame those of us who aren't showing enough promise. Or maybe they are just trying to make sure the river doesn't win too many hands.

When you pass a swimming level you get a badge to sew on your bathing suit. If every square inch of your lower torso isn't covered in as many swatches as the chest of a five-star general you are shunned. Or actually you are worse than shunned: you are required to stay behind the first set of buoys. The set of buoys are where the babies hang out. With their mothers. The eagle-eyed lifeguards can spot badge-less status at twenty paces. At which point they get out their bullhorn: "Would the kid with the red, white and blue bathing suit please move behind the yellow buoys." Sometimes they actually know your name. Or most times they do know my name because they have already tried and failed several times to teach me how to back float.

I slog upstream through the swimming lesson levels until I can officially drop out. The minimum throw-in-the-towel badge is Junior Red Cross, four rungs up the proficiency chart. In our universe, this is equivalent to ditching school at sixteen. Something that can't end well. But Junior Red Cross is enough to gain entry to the second raft. The first raft is in about four feet of water, which makes it entirely useless for jumping off. Unless you like driving your shins up into your thighs. The real raft is the second raft, poised on the edge of the bottomless drop-off. Providing endless opportunity for ways in which to drown.

* * *

The first three levels of swimming proficiency are Minnow, Tadpole and Bantam. I don't know who picked these names or why they thought this was a natural progression, but we start as a Minnow. Let me share some important minnow facts. A minnow is its own species of fish, not just any small fish, and sometimes they aren't actually small at all. Carp are minnows. Goldfish are minnows. Koi ponds are really minnow ponds. There are no minnows in Newfoundland. No, I don't know why.

The first order of business for each swimming lesson is to get in the water. Really get into the water, like past our ankles. Betsy, the swimming teacher, says, "It's nice once you're in!" with the kind of manic enthusiasm that doesn't fool me. I already can't feel my toes. If there is such a thing as water frostbite, I have it. We make a forced march to the string of yellow buoys, which gets us into water just below our bums. "Let's all join hands in a circle!" Betsy enthuses. "Hen, chicken, turkey, DUCK!" When she gets to the "duck" part, we're all supposed to bend our knees and dunk ourselves in the water. Betsy isn't as dumb as she looks. Even if you happen to be less than fully onboard with the duck part of the program, all it takes is for a critical mass of kids to blindly follow Betsy off the cliff for the rest of us to get pulled down below water level.

Once we have a firm grasp on how to put our faces in the water with minimal sputtering, we move on to Tadpole status. Despite this promotion, we remain in the shallows by the shore, probably to lull us into a false sense of security that the river is two feet deep with a soft sandy bottom all the way over to the Quebec side. The main goal of Tadpole is to learn how to kick your legs and move your arms at the same time. Tadpoles, by definition, don't have arms or legs because they're frog larvae. If they had arms and legs they would be frogs, if you call their front appendages arms. But I do figure out how to master lying in twenty-four inches of water, moving my completely emergent appendages in unison, and make a triumphant move on to Bantam.

I will concede that Minnow and Tadpole have some sort of naming logic because they are both aquatic things, but Bantam makes absolutely no sense at all. A bantam is a miniature fowl. A petite chicken. A small flightless bird. To further add to the lack of logic, Bantam is where we master the fine art of the dog paddle. If you are not familiar with the dog paddle, it is most accurately described as the best way to use the most energy to make the least amount of forward progress. I took to the dog paddle like a chicken to water. A chihuahua could swim circles around me. But almost anyone, even kids with my talent for sinking, can make it through Bantam. Especially if you spread it out over at least two summers.

After graduation from the swimming minor leagues, Junior Red Cross is in my cross hairs. Junior Red Cross is an entirely different kettle of pickerel. Because Junior Red Cross involves actual swimming with actual swimming strokes.

Like moving from watching mixed martial arts on TV to signing up for the main card in Las Vegas. And perhaps most importantly, Junior Red Cross requires mastering the art of not drowning. If you manage to drown yourself, you are definitely not getting the badge.

There are two ways to not drown. Actually, there are probably more than two ways, including not going in the water in the first place, but we have to learn two ways and prove they work. One of them is drownproofing. The theory of drownproofing is that the majority of us are inherently buoyant if we have air in our lungs. The thing about theories is that they can be disproven. In drownproofing, you inhale a bunch of air and just hang around in the water with your hands and feet dangling like a jellyfish, bobbing up and down in the not-so-gentle swells, waiting casually to be rescued in a day or two. My lungs do not get the memo. All my drownproofing practice does is give me a great view of the bottom of the river, or it would be a great view if I could open my eyes under water. But I do sort of figure out how to tread water. Me one. Drowning zero.

Swimming test day is always at the end of August, when the water temperature starts to feel warmer than the air. Note that this says more about the air temperature than the water temperature. No test day worth its while has anything less than rampant white caps and three-foot swells.

I line up on the pier with everyone else attempting to join the second raft club, ready to jump in the water to demonstrate my mastery of the breast stroke, side stroke and back stroke, prior to the grand finale of treading water for three minutes. The pier is a slab of concrete supported by cribs filled with rocks. We aren't allowed on the pier except for test days or lesson days that require jumping in the water.

The waves crash over the edge, making the surface slick and slimy. I am freezing even though I'm not wet yet. I wear a Speedo tank suit with red, white and blue stripes, just like every other girl. Speedos are all the rage in 1968 but the catalogue only has one colour that fits preteens. Speedos make you look like a badass swimmer. Unfortunately, I am disguised as a rock in feather clothing.

Cathy, the swimming test officiant, blows her whistle. She tells us to stride jump into the water and start swimming towards the raft. "I need two laps of each stroke," she says. "Don't even think about trying to touch bottom. If you touch bottom you're going to do three extra laps. Have fun out there!"

The stride jump is a proven method to enter the water without dunking your head. I scissor my legs and arms in impeccable stride jump form and sink up to my eyeballs, first inhaling water through my mouth, which has opened in horror, then my nose, which has helpfully kicked into gear to counteract the lack of air in my lungs. But maybe that drownproofing thing has something to it after all, because once I go limp, I reach the surface with enough of my wits to start flailing and sputtering my way through some facsimile of the required strokes. Cathy is just joking about the touching the bottom thing. I'm a good ten feet from the bottom. I know this because I tried. At least I don't get roped into the extra laps.

Despite the promise of the Speedo, I am a master of water resistance in all senses of the meaning. By the time I get back to the designated water treading area, everyone else is already shivering on shore under encroaching thunder clouds. Cathy is so exasperated she puts her stop watch on thirty seconds and calls it a day. In my own defence, thirty seconds is at least ten seconds beyond my personal best. Maybe I have channelled the power of the Speedo after all. I pass the test and snatch the badge out of her hand like a pebble from my karate sensei. I never take another lesson.

Kind of like the person that graduates last in medical school and still gets to call herself a doctor, for every summer after that I hang out on the second raft with Senior Red Cross kids, Bronze Medallion kids and even Royal Lifesaving kids. There is no third raft.

9

Come One, Come All

We head off to visit Expo 67 as our summer vacation trip, partly because we can stay with my maternal grandparents. They live in the part of Quebec that snuggles up against the New York border, like Siamese twins joined at the hip. Here, the invisible line between countries is as porous as a sieve. The border guards ask how the blue paint on the barn is holding up and remind you to pick up extra milk because your sister is visiting next week. Most of the anglophone farm families have been planted here so long that some of them ended up American, when the powers that be finally got around to deciding there should be a country called Canada. They are steadfastly and unapologetically unilingual, although exceptions can be made when buying patate frites from the itinerant food truck or going to the depanneur to pick up some dubious wine for a fancy Sunday dinner.

My grandparents live in a mill town that no longer has a mill, with an army base that was mothballed after World War II, and when you ask for directions through town they tell you to turn right just past where the Woolworths used to be. It's on the shore of the Chateauguay River, which sludges its way without much sense of urgency towards Montreal, fifty-five miles away. And that's where we're headed to see the biggest exposition in the history of the world.

The house where my grandparents live is older than they are. Old enough to have a back stairway that leads from the maid's room to the kitchen. There is no maid anymore. I like the back stairs because they're narrow and steep and if I sit on the edge of the top step just right, I can push off and bump down to the bottom, push the door open with my feet and slide all the way across the kitchen linoleum. This makes my grandmother shriek and clutch her pearls. She wears pearls every waking hour and probably every sleeping hour too. But my grandmother is happy to have kids on hand, otherwise who would put colour in the margarine? The Quebec dairy farmers hate margarine. Well, actually, everyone hates margarine, but it's cheaper than butter. Just like powdered milk is cheaper than fresh milk. For some reason cheap food is all the rage in the 1960s.

Margarine comes in a flat plastic pouch and looks like a slab of shortening with a dab of bright orange in the middle about the size of a penny. This is the colour packet. Margarine is not allowed to be sold already coloured because people might mistake it for butter. That is, until they actually eat it. The butter decoy is unmasked when I squish the button of colour into the white non-animal fat with my thumbs to create a pleasing neon orange spread. Even my dad, who grew up on a dairy farm, eats margarine. Space age food rules.

My grandparents are not coming with us to Expo. "I have to stake up the raspberries," my grandpa says. "No time to waste on a summer fair." Grandpa wears a white dress shirt and his old suit pants when he works in the garden. He's a retired lawyer. Frivolous is not in his lexicon. He has never heard of paisley.

* * *

It's high August and the pavement is already beginning to shimmer as my family shuffles through the Expo 67 gates with the other million people who have the same idea, a crowd that's ten-to-the-power-of-five times the population of my town. We're given fake red passports with empty pages for the fake stamps we'll get as we visit each "country." This turns out to be the largest attendance day of the fair, a sweaty mass of legs in ill-advised miniskirts, golf-appropriate plaid shorts and modest pink skorts ready to meet the manufactured international world with our bogus passports. I am in awe of the swell of humanity, like an amorphous blanket of DNA that incubates the possibility of anonymity. My little brother clings to my mother's hand, terrified he'll be swept away and get lost. What a baby. My other brother and I run ahead towards the space age buildings. The Jetsons probably live here. There's a monorail and everything. I want to live here forever.

The real reason to go to Expo is La Ronde, the amusement park. There are the usual things like a Ferris wheel and a merry-go-round and the swings that whip you around a pole, but also new-fangled scare-mobiles like the Gyrotron. The Gyrotron ride is a cross between a roller coaster and a funhouse. It lives inside a white pyramid with an exoskeleton that looks like someone started to put up scaffolding and forgot to stop. I line up for the ride with my two brothers and wait for the empty chairs to emerge from the end of a dark tunnel and circle back to the entrance. I don't remember any adults being involved and the concept of "you must be this tall to ride" does not yet exist, but if it did my little brother would be about six inches shy of legal. Our turn. We get into what looks like a chairlift that has a bench seat and a place to rest your feet, only mine don't reach that far. A bar swings down from overhead and sort of latches in front of us, at least half-an-arm's length from my waist. We're sitting in our usual back-seat-of-the-car configuration: me and my older brother on the outside and my baby brother between us. In the car, this is to create a buffer so that Michael and I don't poke each other too much and to provide easy access to the windows when either of us needs to barf. I hope this ride does not involve too much barfing, but better to be safe.

The premise of the Gyrotron ride is a trip to outer space followed by a journey to the centre of the earth where a fire-breathing monster lies in wait to do some sort of damage. In the 1960s this makes total sense. Any imagining of what happens in space and what happens after returning from space is perfectly reasonable because after all, dogs and people have circled the earth. It also puts some backstory on a typical roller coaster: there's now a sensible reason why we're going up and down. We chug slowly on an incline in the dark, on our way to see what life is like on Jupiter or Mars. Space junk zips past us, accompanied by flashing red strobe lights, pretending to be rocket exhaust, I'm guessing. Or maybe the designer of the ride just thinks strobe lights are cool. We then plunge towards the face of the earth and I start sliding forward, slipping under the "safety" bar. It's dark so I can't quite see what's happening to everyone else, but I can feel my little brother slithering off the front of the chair, too. Maybe this is how the ride is supposed to work, but I really hope not. I pry one hand off the railing that's keeping me from a crash landing on the innards of the Gyrotron and grab the neck of his t-shirt just as his legs meet thin air. My knuckles are bloodless and I can't feel my fingers. I hope they're still clutching cotton. The ride finally hits bottom and the underground monster does its scary best, which is no match for the chair that brought us here. I have no fingernails left on the hand that's not welded to the chair's railing. We arrive back out from the tunnel, blinking in the daylight, with no adrenaline left. In one fell swoop my brother loses his fear of getting lost. I guess a near-death experience has some redeeming qualities.

The Expo pavilions are pretty boring. I think Walt Disney stole the idea for the Epcot international area from Expo (which, in case you have never been, is also pretty boring). They are feats of mid-century modern architecture meant to reflect the chosen theme of the nation in question, usually with a movie projected on a three-hundred-and-sixty-degree screen that requires holding your neck at an unnatural angle, and a gift shop where you can buy keepsake trinkets (Russian dolls made in China). However, there are some must-see architectural destinations on our list, like the USSR, U.S. and Ontario.

The USSR's contribution is a brutalist marvel celebrating the 1917 revolution and the thoroughly modern progress of communism: unlimited potatoes, unlimited vodka, communal apartments and hot water as a shared utility that can conveniently be turned off in the summer. Atomic energy and the space race figure prominently, especially the fact that Yuri Gagarin, not Alan Shepard, first saw our little blue planet from outer space. The U.S. has a geodesic dome that stares down the Russian contingent from across a muddy canal. It's kind of all form and no function, which goes with its theme of "creative America." Andy Warhol's soup cans and Roy Lichtenstein's tearful comic book damsels in romantic distress are prominently displayed. I don't know how they figured out how to hang them on concave walls but I guess if you can build a two-hundred-foot-high dome, a feat that's never been attempted before, how you attach art to the walls is the least of your problems. Unfortunately, the mini-rail transit system that schleps guests around the grounds goes right through the centre of the dome at about halfway up the twenty stories, which does not help my Gyrotron flashbacks, but it's the shortest route to the Ontario pavilion. And that's where we're headed next, after lunch.

We're standing in a line-up for the exotic Pepsi restaurant. We're supposed to meet my dad at the beer garden in half an hour. "I really have to pee," Stephen announces.

"Oh for Pete's sake. We just passed a bathroom on the way here. All right, let's go back," says my mother, as she yanks Stephen out of the line by his wrist. "You two just stay in line and wait here. And don't move."

"But what if the line moves ahead? Are we allowed to move then?" I ask innocently.

"Stop being so ridiculous! Honestly, I don't know why we brought you kids here in the first place. We'll be back from the bathroom in a sec," my mother says.

I'm not so sure about that. In my experience a "sec" means anywhere from five minutes to five hours. Neither of us has a watch. Michael and I inch forward in the line, wiping our sweaty palms on our t-shirts. At least 1,200 secs later, I finally see my mother's blue paisley dress heading our way. We're almost at the front of the line.

"What do you kids want to eat?" asks my mother. I don't know why she bothers asking. I'm having a grilled cheese sandwich. Michael's having a hamburger. Stephen's having a hotdog. And one orange pop, one root beer and one Pepsi. This never changes.

We make our way to the beer garden and find my dad parked under an awning with two Löwenbräu in front of him. My mother smiles and waves. "Kids, go and hang out at the children's area while dad and I have lunch." The beer garden has thoughtfully provided a place for parents to offload their offspring. No supervision involved, of course.

* * *

Of course, we know all about Ontario already since we've lived there for seven years now. The Ontario pavilion has granite rocks hived off the Canadian Shield to clamber up and fake robots to tell us about the careers we should pursue to be part of Ontario's future of the future. "Miss Science" wants us to be food scientists and invent a better form of shelf-stable cheese. "Businessman" (who is clearly a man but doesn't get to be "Mr. Businessman") thinks fine jobs in the field of commerce are door-to-door encyclopedia sales and TV repair. But we're not here for these silly distractions. We're here for the movie *A Place to Stand*, an eighteen-minute video montage of all things Ontario. Logging. Mining. Making steel. Railways. All of the things that are well positioned to form a robust economy in the twenty-first century. And all of the careers the fake robots are prepared to discuss. We're here for the movie because our town has a cameo role.

Oddly, the film opens with a shot of a guy in a pink short-sleeve shirt, smoking and drinking what looks like a Big Gulp of Coke, or maybe it's an extra-large double-double coffee or maybe a rye and ginger. However, it recovers nicely with a close-up of a trillium, then two trilliums, then a sea of trilliums, Ontario's official flower. But we are not here to see trilliums, which literally grow like weeds in our backyard. We are here to see our swimming beach and bike parking lot have their fifteen minutes (or to be honest, fifteen seconds) of fame. I don't know how or why our town got to be part of the photoshoot, but one day last summer a film crew arrived and we had our close up moment, along with a temporary reprieve from swimming lessons. At about the halfway mark of the movie, here we all are, kids blanketing the sand like a colony of beached beavers, our hundreds of bikes neatly parked behind the lifeguard shack. I'm convinced my blue CCM glider with the purple handlebar streamers plays a cameo role in the second bike rack from the left. But then again, they're all blue CCM gliders. The only kind of bike at Canadian Tire. *A Place to Stand* went on to win Best Live Action Short at the 1968 Academy Awards. My bicycle wants to thank all the little people that made this possible.

Despite the international theme, Expo was pretty white-bread. You could barely buy brown bread in 1967 and garlic was still very ethnic, although garlic powder was allowed (because powdered anything was allowed and even encouraged). Each pavilion had "hostesses" that were supposed to represent something about the national culture, but my recollection is that the only variation in costuming was the colour of their miniskirts and pillbox hats.

But I got to be there. I couldn't make sense of it all yet, but my brain synapses were sizzling. Maybe there's a world that doesn't involve needing to learn math or science. A world where maybe everyone doesn't know who you are and who your parents are. A world where maybe everyone doesn't see what you're doing that you shouldn't be doing or what you're not doing that you should be doing.

10

Math Doubles Down

It's still 1967 for a few more months, so there's still time to tidy up those remaining centennial projects and make it under the wire. The big project for the town comes in well ahead of the deadline. It's a boulder by the river, shaped like a squished, three-dimensional trapezoid, with a flat face that has the requisite plaque on it that says pretty much what every other requisite plaque says. Something about the past hundred years and the next hundred years and probably something about flying cars and living on the moon. There's also the mandatory time capsule just below the rock, encased in reinforced concrete that can withstand a nuclear winter. It likely contains things that are not expected to still exist in 2067: Tang, a two-dollar bill, a Beatles album (sans record player), a TV guide, an Eaton's catalogue, and last week's crop of molybdenum-99. They were right about all of these things except for the Tang.

The invisible divide between the east and west side of town dissolves when the kids from our two elementary schools converge at Keys Public School for grade 7 and 8. At Keys, I have a homeroom with a hybrid group of some kids I know from my old school and new ones from Morison school way on the other side of town. This is both weird and exciting. It's a bubble of unfamiliarity in a world where everything is known. My homeroom teacher is Miss Bell. Miss Bell is so recently out of teacher's college she's as green as a maple tree in the spring. "Guess how old I am?" she asks, this activity apparently being much more important than delving into grade 7 academics. After all, we have the whole year to deal with minor details like learning something.

Somebody at the back of the room shouts out, "Thirty?"

This does not impress Miss Bell. "I'm twenty-two, you dummies!" she shouts. What a relief, since it makes her at least old enough to babysit us. Miss Bell decides to change tack in her getting-to-know-you pursuit. "Whose father is a doctor?" she asks. Half the class raises their hands, even though only Karen's dad would qualify if a pilot asks if there is a doctor on the plane. As part of her orientation briefing when she got to town, Miss Bell must have learned the fun fact that Deep River has more PhDs per capita than anywhere else on earth and is putting this knowledge under the microscope. I don't think Miss Bell is going to fit in around here. Her half-life will probably be measured in nanoseconds.

Luckily, we don't have to spend all day with Miss Bell, only for gym and social studies. We have a subject timetable and rotate classes, almost like teenagers, when a buzzer sounds at the end of the period. Each period is fifty-five minutes with five minutes left over before the hour so we can change classes. We have five periods a day and seven subjects, not counting gym, so we don't get every class every day. But some subjects are more important than others. French gets one period a week, which means we have to wait a whole seven days in suspense before we learn the true fate of the little dog Pitou and the results of the strike. Why it's considered necessary for us to learn the French verb for "to strike" before, say, the verb "to eat" is not clear. We also learn how to discuss waiting for an elevator en francais (I have never been in an elevator), and the important distinction between a holiday and a vacation. A holiday is when the government gives you the day off, a vacation is when you go somewhere, but strangely there's no word for going somewhere on a holiday, so please don't do that if you speak French.

In contrast, math gets six periods per week. And if you do the math, you'll figure out that sometimes that means two math classes a day. Unfortunately, when math shows up twice it's always twinned with itself. The dreaded "double math." Our school is named after Dr. Keys, one of the scientists who invented the town. He has a school named after him even though he isn't dead yet. Maybe we double down on the math so that we don't sully Dr. Keys's good name by failing to meet the qualifications required to become nuclear physicists. Except we're only in grade 7.

* * *

"Okay, class," Mr. McKay, our math teacher, announces. "I want you to determine the relationship between the area of a parallelogram and the area of a trapezoid by composing a parallelogram from congruent trapezoids."

There's a seven-foot-long slide rule hanging above the blackboard. It looks like a regular ruler that's had a tragic horizontal accident in two places. It's been put back together but now has to live its life with a middle that's permanently disconnected from its upper and lower sides, however, this leads to a much higher calling than just measuring stuff. Buzz

Aldrin took one to the moon, for crying out loud. But even that doesn't impress me much. The slide rule is a menace of logarithmic scales that are supposed to make it easier to multiply and divide large numbers. There's a bunch of its ten-inch babies at the front of the room in a box that probably used to hold the Cuisenaire rods. A slide rule doesn't know how to add or subtract, so it loses even more marks for that. The giant slide rule is only for use in the classroom, though. When Mr. McKay is at the grocery store and needs to calculate pi to the fortieth decimal, he uses the one in the leather holster attached to his belt.

Today is not learn slide rule day, though. This endless expanse of math is devoted to learning base eight. Near as I can tell, base eight is numbers for people who can't count to ten.

Apparently, English weights and measures, which no one anywhere at any time in history has been able to understand, are largely an octal system. And maybe that's why base eight is being foisted upon us: to help calculate how many bushels in a peck and acres in a half-section. All practical modern skills to take us into the nether regions of the twentieth century.

"To convert integer decimals to octal, divide the original number by the largest possible power of eight and divide the remainders by successively smaller powers of eight until the power is one." Mr. McKay drones on.

"Happy days are here again, double math time's here again, let's sing a song of cheer again, double math, double math, double math, is here again," sings my inside voice. I am tap dancing double time on a Broadway stage. The crowd is going wild. The leading man looks just like Davy Jones from the Monkees.

I wake up with Mr. McKay saying, "Your homework is due tomorrow and the test is on Tuesday," as he wipes the instructions for the assignment off the board. At least there's a sock hop this week.

* * *

We have a real gym in a brand-new extension to the school. No more phys ed in the classroom aisles, featuring jumping jacks and squats in our school clothes. Our new gym has a fancy wooden gym floor with built-in lines for volleyball and basketball. Preparation for gym consists of swapping your existing socks for gym socks or if you are a girl, putting gym socks over the feet of your stockings. The socks are because of the shiny floor. The socks must be white. The gym floor is not for feet and especially not for shoes. Even gym shoes. We cannot besmirch Dr. Keys's nice new floor.

For some reason our gym does not have much of a change room, just some benches and hooks in an alcove. So much for ditching the school clothes. I guess the theory is twelve-year-olds don't actually sweat. Not that we do too much that would involve sweat. Except for dodgeball. The objective of dodgeball is to obliterate all players on the opposing team, and my classmates take that mandate seriously. Miss Bell counts us off into teams. "One, two, one, two, one, two. All the ones move to the left side of the gym and the twos to the right side!" Each team has a random number of boys and girls with no attempt to balance things out. In grade 7, levelling the playing field means making sure there aren't too many girls on one side or the other, not because the girls are a handicap but because they are at least a head taller and twenty pounds heavier than most of the boys.

My strategy is to get eliminated as soon as possible so I can go sit on a bench and read *A Wrinkle in Time* for the bazillionth time. I love this book because it takes me far away from here. I want to travel between universes with Meg Murry, not hang out in a smelly gym. I move forward into the line of fire and try to anticipate the trajectory of the ball about to be launched at us by team two. It comes within a whisper of my shoulder, and, with skill worthy of a World Cup soccer player, I take a dive and lie on my back. Miss Bell blows the whistle and sends me off to recuperate. Barb gives me a dirty look. "No fair! That was fake, she isn't out!" she snarls. Barb likes gym. Barb likes to win even if it's just stupid dodgeball. Barb would be the captain of dodgeball team one if there was a captain. Barb is always the captain. But I've fooled Miss Bell and that's the main thing. Fooling Miss Bell is about as easy as falling asleep in math class. Gym recess begins for me and I get back to the world of fifth-dimension travel and planet Camazotz.

* * *

Every so often we have a sock hop. A sock hop is a middle school dance. The attire for a sock hop is exactly the same as for gym class because sock hops happen in the gym, immediately after school. There is no dressing up for a sock hop, we wear our normal school clothes. The gym looks exactly like it does on any other day, except for the twisted streamers hanging from the florescent light fixtures that blaze like they're illuminating a deep woods airstrip. The social committee puts up the streamers and gets to leave class early to complete the party makeover. I'd volunteer for the social committee, but sock hops rarely happen on double-math day so the appeal is less than compelling. Sock hops are pretty much like dodgeball, but without the balls or teams. Or that's not quite true. We do still have teams. Our two teams are divided into girls and boys, who line up on opposite sides of the gym. The girls close rank into a circle, while the boys slouch against the cinderblock walls, looking bored. Jimmy takes some jacks out of his pocket and a bunch of boys start an impromptu game. The jacks skitter across the floor and catch Mr. Pearson's attention. Mr. Pearson teaches English and is one of our sock hop chaperones. Mr. Pearson does not have a hard job in this instance. He blows his whistle. "You boys stop scratching the floor! You aren't supposed to be having fun here. This is the gym! Now smarten up!" The boys laugh behind his back and switch to throwing spit balls at each other.

At the end-of-year dance we have live music, but in between we have a DJ. Mikey is the DJ today. We all bring 45s to school for him to play. I contribute Herman's Hermits and the Zombies, with the plastic adapter already installed in the hole in the middle. He loads the turntable with a stack of records and moves the needle to the bottom one. It makes a scratchy noise before the Beatles start singing "Yellow Submarine," sounding like they are under water and swimming in slow motion. Brief intermission while Mikey switches the record player from 33 rpm to 45 and tapes a penny to the arm of the needle to stop it from skipping. The records drop about every three minutes: "There's a Kind of Hush," "Penny Lane," "Ferry Cross the Mersey," "Ruby Tuesday." A who's who of the British Invasion.

The one thing that's true about every sock hop is that nobody ever dances. There might be some minor foot shuffling and finger snapping but absolutely nothing that would equate to a Twist or a Frug or even a Monkey and especially nothing that would rely on a partner. The sexes remain in their two solitudes, the girls giggling and the boys sullen. I am not sure what the point of a sock hop is except to listen to other kids' records. But I would never miss one. We are part of the 1960s but not quite of them. Too young for the summer of love. Too young to hitchhike across Canada. Too young to grow Fu Manchu mustaches. But we can listen to the music and turn it up so loud it gives Mr. Pearson a headache. And there is nothing he can do about it. He doesn't know how to work the sound system. That's because it's not as complicated as a slide rule.

11

Seeing the Forest

Many people profess to live in the middle of nowhere, or on the edge of nowhere or if maybe not exactly in the middle of nowhere, they can see it from there. So I can't claim sole custody of the nowhere experience. However, there is a limited set of people that can attest and affirm that they live in the official middle of nowhere. Most right-thinking people would agree the official middle of nowhere is the place inhabited by the official forest. That is, the twenty-five thousand acres of white pine, red pine, aspen and birch trees that comprise the Petawawa Research Forest, a.k.a. the forestry.

The forestry is a popular school field trip from the town of Deep River, especially in the waning months of the school year when pretty much all there is to be learned has already been learned and is more than ready to be forgotten over the summer. Please note, the fact the forestry is at the top of the outdoor-learning hit parade says more about the availability of suitable destinations within day-trip distance from town than about the wonders of the forestry itself. Not that there's anything wrong with trees, except when you've reached peak tree saturation, as you do when you live in a town that barely staves off the trees that surround it on all sides. I already know pretty much all there is to know about trees. I can tell an aspen from a silver birch, even in winter when they look pretty much the same (just look at the bark, does it peel or not?). I can tell a red pine from a white pine (just look at the needles, are there two or five per bunch?). I can detect poison ivy at twenty-paces and I can mostly find edible berries. Or more correctly, find berries that on average, will be mostly edible. But never mind, forestry trip it is. We load onto the school bus with Mr. Miller who teaches grade 8 science. The terrain on the highway towards Petawawa mostly consists of tall, skinny pines growing out of sand that's covered in whatever ground cover grows on sand. I see trees and sand. Sand and trees. And crows the size of my little brother that perch on the pointy tips of the pines, bending the tops southward. Eyeing our bus like it's full of lunch.

"Now pay attention to the topography, you kids," Mr. Miller says. But we're too busy bartering our Monkees trading cards, the ones that come with the rectangular slab of inedible gum. I like the one with Micky Dolenz on the beach with a guitar, but I'm not going to trade my picture of Davy Jones in the swimming pool for it, even if there's a dumb girl in the background. Besides, why does Micky Dolenz have a guitar? He's the drummer, for poop's sake. Maybe it was too hard to carry drums to the beach for the photo or maybe drums don't work so good on sand. But you can't fool me, Micky, because anyhow, I'm keeping the cards I have. So I slide them back into my green science scribbler to keep them in as pristine condition as possible, a goal that's pretty much in the rear-view mirror. I have an official Monkees shirt at home that I wear to school when I know it's a sock hop day. It has a white, rounded, oblong collar that's called a "dog ear collar" because it's supposed to look like a floppy dog ear. I don't know about that part because I don't have a dog and nobody I know has a dog and in fact, I have never seen a dog in town. I have no idea why, except maybe we live above the dog line. The shirt part is green and blue paisley, because green and blue are Davy's favourite colours. According to *Tiger Beat*. I don't have much to wear it with. Only my green and blue plaid skirt. But I'm sure Davy would approve. At least I'm pretty sure he looks down with adoration at my outfit choice from the pull-out *Tiger Beat* centrefold tacked up on my bedroom wall. Don't worry. He's fully clothed right down to the puka shell necklace showing in the opening of his weird red shirt that has a rectangular placket with two rows of four buttons. I know what a placket is because Mrs. Graham in home ec taught us how to make one. Davy's belt buckle is the size of the saucers that go under the tea cups my mother uses for bridge club. But with no flowers on it.

Mr. Miller tells us to look out the left side of the bus. "See those things that look like giant moguls? Those are sand dunes from the bottom of the Champlain Sea. From ten thousand years ago when the glaciers retreated," he says. I wonder if they made kids learn to swim in the Champlain Sea. The part right beside the highway that was cut away to put the road through reveals the dunes in cross-section, an undulating row of prehistoric camel humps. How come I've never noticed this before? I write this in my notebook just in case it's on the test. And every time I'm on this road after that I look for the disembodied dromedaries and will them telepathically to reveal their ice age secrets.

* * *

The forestry has a fire tower because, well, forest. Fire towers need to be taller than the trees, so you will always find them on the top of a hill. There's one on Mount Martin, on the Quebec side of the river too, but I've never been to that one. This one's probably better anyway, because it's in the official forest, and official stuff is supposed to be better. Like an official Monkees shirt, not the pretend ones you can get at Woolworths in Pembroke. "Single file, class," Mr. Miller says, as we hike up the path to the base of the tower, like there would actually be room for more than single file unless you want to scrape your legs on the raspberry bushes. The tower is set in a clearing that forms a miniature, circular firebreak. The base of the tower is four metal legs that taper towards a pyramid point at the top and enclose a switch-backed stairway that leads up to the lookout cabin. I'm not so keen about heights but I get swept along with the rest of the class like a row of lemmings, but in this case going up the cliff instead of down. "Groups of ten, please," Mr. Miller says. "We don't want to test the strength of the floor too much."

I squish into the first group and get in line between two boys so I can shield myself from most aspects of the upward journey. I close my eyes and move my feet up the steps of the ladder whenever the kid in front of me moves. If I fall down, I'm taking them all down with me. After about three hundred hours by my reckoning, with a near-death experience every time I lift a foot off a rung, we reach the trap door at the bottom of the lookout hut. Mr. Miller hauls me up and I cram in. As long as I keep my eyes closed, I'm good. Everyone except me takes turns squinting through the lookout thing, which is kind of like binoculars but attached to a pole so the viewfinder can swivel around to see the whole landscape. "Where there's smoke, there's fire," Mr. Miller intones with great gravitas. "All it would take is one lightning strike on a dry day like today and we'd all be goners." I'm about to put up my hand and ask about the firebreak and whether or not it would keep our town safe, but I think the better of it. What if he says it won't keep us safe? Anyhow, why would there be a thunderstorm on a bright blue day like today?

Going down the fire tower ladder is better than up, as long as I don't look up. Or down. At least gravity is on my side and every step takes me closer to the ground. I make sure I'm just above another girl so everyone can look up her skirt instead of mine. I wish I'd figured that out on the way up. I guess there are no girl forest rangers, because who would want to climb up and down a ladder in a skirt all day? I'm not signing up for fire tower duty any time soon.

We follow a path made from wood chips back to the ranger station, wood chips being an endlessly renewable resource in the forestry. *The Forest Rangers* show that's on TV on Saturdays just before dinner has fire towers and a ranger station too, but all of that's just pretend. We all make fun of *The Forest Rangers* because it's like a fairy-tale representation of life in the actual forest, but we all watch it every week without fail. The forest rangers on TV live in a town called Indian River, which is supposed to be just north of Barry's Bay, which is a good eighty miles south of us. In television-land, Indian River is way up north in the bush. I've been to Barry's Bay and no way there's a place called Indian River. The kids that are junior forest rangers never wear bug spray and never get bitten by bugs. They all have walkie-talkies that seem to work in dense forest, even though walkie-talkies need a reliable AM frequency. We know this is doo-doo because we can't even pull in an AM radio signal until after dark when we can finally capture stations, but they're from somewhere in Minnesota or Michigan and cut in and out. *Just wrote me a letter ... ticket to ride ... devil ... all the greatest hits.* But the junior forest rangers have official ranger t-shirts and a Smokey the Bear flag flying over their fort, which looks like a real fort with turrets and everything, whereas our firebreak forts can barely manage walls. So what if it's filmed just outside of Toronto, a six hour drive south, and the television forest rangers have never really seen a real forest? The junior forest rangers get to do cool stuff with no adults around. Come to think of it, kind of like we do. But we get to do it for real.

Mr. Miller points out the birches and aspens. Yeah, yeah, we already know all that. "Aspens are only found in places with cold winters," he says, stating the obvious. "But did you know, an aspen can breathe through its bark so it can grow even in the winter without leaves?" I did not know that, but I do know that when the aspen leaves shake like a swimmer emerging from the Ottawa River and you can see the pale green underside, you'd better head for cover because there's bad weather coming in from the west.

We head back towards the field trip bus. Richard lags behind, lifting small rocks in hope of snagging a salamander to bring back to class. It's always under the last rock you pick up. Just before we get to the lay-by where our ride is parked, Richard squeals with glee. "Got one! Got one! But it only has three legs!! Mr. Miller, Mr. Miller, can we take him home?"

Mr. Miller shoos the rest of us onto the bus and goes to examine Richard's treasure. The bus lists to the right as the whole class crowds over, leaning our heads out of the top part of the windows to see what's going on. "First of all," he says, "that's a girl because it's big and has small lips." Salamanders have lips? "Second, her missing arm will grow back." Gross, I think. "Sure, Richard," says Mr. Miller. "Stick her in your lunch box for now, and she can live in the terrarium at the back of the classroom." What will we feed her? Do salamanders like leftover banana, I wonder? Why on earth would someone want banana in the first place? Just the smell of it makes me want to barf. But a gimpy salamander also makes me a little queasy.

We take a highly democratic vote on the bus to name our new science experiment. "Sally! Mandy! Ally! Gator! Davy Jones!" That last one is me. I get vetoed on my choice because it's not deemed appropriate for a girl amphibian. Sally it is. I wonder if she learned to swim in the Ottawa River? If so, she's okay with me.

* * *

I know Mr. Morris mostly from choir. Mr. Morris is mean. At our choir rehearsal for the recital, he told us he'd stop our performance if we came in too early after the first verse of "I've Got Spurs That Jingle Jangle Jingle." "There's a rest here, people! The composer would not put a rest in if he didn't mean there should be a rest! A rest means a rest! You stop when there's a rest. Am I making myself clear?" Mr. Morris seems a little exasperated.

Sure enough, I'm on stage at the recital, front and centre in the soprano section, wearing my best white shirt and requisite navy skirt, when some dork in the back comes in early. What an amateur! Mr. Morris brings his conductor fingers into train wreck mode and we grind to a halt. "At practice I said I'd stop them if they didn't do it right," he explains to the parents in the audience, "so we're going to start over and do it until we get it right." Luckily, my parents are curling and miss the endless loop of the junior high choir going not-so-merrily along.

Mr. Morris is our chaperone for the 1960s version of take-your-kid-to-work day. Take-your-kid-to-work day is a homogeneous activity in our world, so for our next field trip we wait until the AECL buses arrive back in town mid-morning, and my entire class piles on to go see what our dads do all day. Nobody messes with Mr. Morris. That's probably why he's on the field trip to the plant. He'd send any rogue atoms packing long before their electrons could even stop spinning.

Despite the mysterious space age scenarios supplied by my imagination, the guardhouse gate turns out to be the most exciting thing at the plant. The fence has barbed wire just like on *Hogan's Heroes,* and there's a guard in a uniform, except he doesn't have a machine gun. At least I can't see a machine gun. We get off the bus and walk through the gate. Mr. Morris reads our names out and the guard writes them on his official visitor list. That's so he knows that all the kids who came in eventually all make it out, and also so he can put our names on our dosimeter badges. And maybe also so he can tell on us if we steal any molybdenum-99.

A dosimeter badge is a square frame of plastic that holds a special type of photographic film that measures and records radiation exposure from gamma rays, X-rays and beta particles. Good thing all those angles are covered. At the end of our visit, the dosimeters will tell us if we're dead, on our way to deadness or good for another few years of radiation exposure. We can't actually visit the reactors themselves because that would require coveralls that don't come in kid sizes, plus there'd be all that extra time required for the decontamination shower. So we head to the lab where the white-coat scientific stuff takes place.

"And this is where we examine the properties of the '4n + 1' series of nuclear isotopes that are not found in nature, but are created from successive disintegration of uranium-233. It's analogous to the three series of naturally radioactive isotopes that have been long known to result from the disintegration of uranium, thorium and actinium," our tour guide says, in some language that sounds sort of like English, as he points to a microscope. I recognize some of the words. Like "the," "but" and "from." Fascinating. Looks just like Mr. Miller's science room but without the three-legged salamander and in fact, a salamander would have been a nice decorative touch.

None of us see our dads actually at work on this field trip, so that remains a mystery, although I know my dad sometimes works the graveyard night shift because, unlike the rest of us, the reactors need adult supervision in case the atoms decide they are tired of being cooped up and start plotting a midnight escape. "Working the graveyard tonight," he says. "I hope I don't get scared!" I imagine my dad roaming between the headstones in an actual graveyard, wearing one of those miner's hats with a light attached, making sure the dead people don't sit up in their coffins like Dracula, ready to do a zombie walk up the plant road. Now that would be worth a bus ride. This was clearly not, except for the part about being out of the classroom. That's always worth it, even if there's science involved.

12

Fashion Victim

Junior high boys take shop and junior high girls take home ec. The girls never see the inside of a shop class, just what comes out of the shop class: cutting boards for mothers to use in the kitchen, misshapen salad bowls for mothers to use in the kitchen, and wooden spoons for mothers to use in the kitchen. It seems the purpose of shop class is to create things that will eventually be useful to graduates of home ec.

In home ec, girls learn the essence of being a girl: how to cook, clean and sew. We learn to make fried eggs, scrambled eggs, poached eggs, boiled eggs, coddled eggs and omelets, because we don't know which kind of eggs our future husbands will prefer. Apparently, our future husbands will all be fans of broiled grapefruit with brown sugar on top and half a maraschino cherry in the centre, because it is served on the side for every order of eggs du jour. Or maybe the grapefruit is just the stand-in for teaching us how to use the broiler, since I have never in my life encountered a broiled grapefruit outside of the home ec kitchen. Anyhow, I think it would be easier to just find a husband who likes the kind of eggs I can make (hard boiled) as opposed to the other way around. I'm certainly not going to look for one who likes porridge, although we learn to make that too. Breakfast is the most important meal of the day.

Lunch transforms itself into "luncheon" in the home ec room. A luncheon must involve either an elaborate cold plate or a tiny, perfect version of a hot meal. Sandwiches belong at afternoon tea only. I learn how to make aspic and the science behind floating things in Jell-O, because fruit, vegetables, eggs, meat or anything vaguely edible encased in flavoured gelatin are the hallmark of a luncheon. "Now girls, remember you cannot use pineapple, papaya or mango," says Mrs. Graham, "because the enzymes interfere with the collagen proteins. Can anyone name the amino acids found in collagen?" We can't even get away from science in home ec. And what are mangos and papayas? They have certainly never darkened the door of the local A&P and I've barely even seen a pineapple with its clothes on. I am about to ask Mrs. Graham what a mango looks like, but on second thought, I don't need to know, because I have no intention of ever floating anything in Jell-O outside of this room.

We learn to clean the kitchen because only girls would ever be allowed in a kitchen so only girls need to know this. Also, Mrs. Graham gets slave labour to put the kitchen back shipshape before the next class. We do the dishes with Palmolive because it's good for your hands. In fact, it's probably so good for your hands you should soak them in it. That's what they say on TV, anyway. We mop the floor with water and vinegar so the room smells like a fish and chips shop once we're done.

But the real attraction of home ec is sewing. If you can sew, you can make your own clothes with the Simplicity or McCall's patterns they sell at Ritter's fabric store, right in the town shopping plaza. If you don't make your own clothes you're stuck with the blue, pink or green version of the skirts and dresses at Ritter's children's wear store. Either that or get someone's mother to drive you forty miles to Pembroke, if she's not too busy curling or playing bridge.

The fabric store has metal filing cabinets that hold all the patterns and a high table where the pattern books are laid out for perusing. Pattern books are about the size of the Gutenberg Bible, a foot and a half tall and two feet wide and upwards of five hundred pages long. And they are treated with about the same amount of reverence because they hold the key to the kingdom of unlimited fashion. I climb up on a stool and open the cover of the Simplicity book, which is as thick and heavy as our Christmas turkey platter, but instead of holly leaves it's decorated with drawings of women and girls wearing capes, jumpers with patch-pockets on the front, minidresses and skorts, which are a Siamese twin construction of a skirt with shorts underneath, so that you can wear pants without technically wearing pants.

Simplicity patterns are easy, or at least on the easy end of the sewing pattern spectrum. I'm not tackling the Vogue pattern book anytime soon, even if that's the only kind Twiggy wears. Twiggy is the platonic form of swinging '60s femininity, with an androgynous figure and legs that are almost as skinny as mine. This is why I love her. She promises there is a place in the world for skinny, shapeless girls. I flip through the pattern book to the "young misses" section. A young miss is what you are when you have a bust line just like Twiggy's and don't even need darts, except they always make you put in darts. I don't know why there are so many different patterns, since all the minidresses look pretty much the same. Same skirt length. Same A-line shape. The only things that change are the sleeves and the necklines. Maybe not so unlimited fashion after all.

Once you know what style of minidress you want, you write down the pattern number and bring it to the front desk. Retrieving a pattern is like taking the Gutenberg for a spin in the rare-book reading room at the British Museum. First, the clerk writes the pattern number, company name, size and fashion season on a pink index card. Then she takes a key from a large ring hanging on a hook behind the counter and heads to the filing cabinets. She opens the appropriate drawer to locate the pattern number in sequence, pulls out the pattern, and replaces it with the pink card. She walks back to the counter, where she cuts the strip off the back flap of the pattern envelope that holds the duplicate of the pattern number, staples it to a white piece of cardboard and files it in the reorder file. Then the pattern is all mine. If you want to be subversive, when the clerk turns her back during these tasks you can miss-file any remaining copies of the pattern so no one else will have it. I don't know how I know this, because I certainly never did this.

* * *

We sit down to the home ec sewing machines and Mrs. Graham puts us through our paces. First, we make a bobbin. The bobbin thread is the one that goes along the underside of the fabric and keeps the top thread in place. It's kind of important but also pretty much invisible unless you know it exists. The bobbin thread doesn't really need to be the same colour as the main thread and in fact it's better if it isn't because then it's easier to see it when you need to rip your seam out. I am, in fact, highly skilled with a seam ripper.

A seam ripper is a tool that looks like a small screw driver except the "driver" part is like a skinny shark's tooth honed to a razor pinpoint, all the better to yank offending threads into oblivion. I have impaled my palm so many times I can now comfortably use it as a pin cushion.

Today we're making tote bags for our mothers to carry their winter shoes. Or maybe it's for her to carry around her wooden salad bowl. The tote bag has only one piece for the back and one for the front, so there's lots of straight sewing. "Now girls," says Mrs. Graham, "no racing. You do not need to race."

Oh yes, we do. We're like Formula One drivers lined up at the starting gate of the Monaco Grand Prix, barely reining in our engines. Sewing machines are our version of the power tools the boys get to use in shop and we are going to take them on the joy ride we deserve. I stamp my foot down on the pedal that spurs the sewing machine into action. My needle goes up and down so fast it's a blur. I get to the end of the first side of the tote bag, quickly raise the presser foot lever to pivot to the second side and lead-foot my way to the end. The room smells like diesel pumps at a truck stop. Mrs. Graham sees the cloud of sewing machine exhaust wafting towards the ceiling, and yellow-flags us over for a pit stop. "Okay. I think that's quite enough sewing for today," she says. My foot pedal is as hot as the broiler pan and is making weird popping noises. I busy myself with positioning the sewing machine cover and tidying up the thread so Mrs. Graham doesn't notice the melting metal. Maybe I'd better choose a different machine next time. Don't want to risk setting the home ec room on fire without even turning on the stove.

* * *

Just so you know, a miniskirt isn't just any old short skirt. A miniskirt has an official specification as decreed by Mary Quant, and she should know since she is credited with inventing it. Although, in the way of all things that become insanely popular and iconic of an era, many others have stepped up to claim miniskirt inventor status. Anyhow, to be an official miniskirt, the skirt must hit roughly at mid-thigh and can be no longer than four inches below the point at which the upper thigh meets the fleshy bit of the rear end. Every female, regardless of age, wore a miniskirt in the late 1960s. Even my mother. Even her mother. Even Mrs. Graham, who was at least as old as my mother. Because that's all there was in the store and in the pattern books. At least until hot pants showed up, which was an entirely different issue with respect to appropriate attire for women of all ages. But if the fashion industry decreed it, we all wore it.

For some reason, except for very little kids, there was no such thing as tights. Pantyhose hadn't been invented yet, or if it did exist in some space age factory, it was at least three or four years out from mass commercialization and at least five years out from being accessible in the boonies like the Ottawa Valley. So, this is what eight-, nine-, ten-, eleven- and twelve-year-old girls wore: thick stockings held up by garters.

My garter belt is a three-inch band of elastic with four garters in the front and four in the back. It has a tendency to twist into a Pillsbury crescent roll somewhere near my belly button because I have no waist yet to keep my undergarments separated north from south. I have never washed my garter belt and maybe washing it is considered ill-advised because it might ruin the elastic. In any case, it started out white but now is roughly the colour of the dishwater as it leaves the home ec room sink.

My stockings are a straight tube of woven cotton about one-and-a-half times the circumference of my thigh. But at least they are psychedelic purple. The easiest way to get the stockings on is to fasten the tops to the garters first, then pull them on along with the garter belt. I don't think this is the officially sanctioned way to do it. I don't care. The tops of the stockings end about three inches from the apex of my leg, with only an inch worth's margin of error between my skirt hem and my garters. This is where pettipants come in. Pettipants are bloomers that cover the territory between the garter belt and the top of the stockings. The solution for badly planned undergarments is always additional undergarments. Pettipants are a truncated pair of tights cut off at mid-thigh. You would think that if someone could come up with pettipants to mitigate the stocking gap, they could have just continued on and invented the tight. But that did not happen at this point. Pettipants also have stretch lace trim on the leg openings and a smattering of lace across middle of the rear end. This is so that if your miniskirt rides up, like for example, if you have to play dodgeball, or climb up a fire tower ladder, or sit at a desk in a classroom, everyone will see only ladylike lace.

Pettipants come in three colours: baby blue, apple green and hot pink. The pink and blue ones are the most popular so all that's left when I get to Ritter's is the green ones. Which go with nothing. But pettipants are the closest thing I will get to actual pants, skorts notwithstanding, until two years from now.

13

Type Cast

At August's mid-gasp, when you can count the remaining summer holidays on both hands, the list goes up on the front doors of Dr. C. J. Mackenzie High School, the one and only high school for sixty miles as the highway flies. The list tells you what homeroom you will be in and who else will be in it. The only kids who actually care about this are those of us starting grade 9. The high school building sits between the middle school and my grade school. I've spent seven years looking at both its east- and west-side profile, but now it's time to move our relationship to the next level. It looks like every other high school in existence in 1969, which I would know if I had ever seen another high school. It has a football field with goal posts at either end, ringed with a cinder-surfaced track, a parking lot where the cool kids hang out to smoke, and halls lined with lockers, ringed with photos of athletic teams and Ontario Scholars showing the advancement of female hairdos and male hair lengths over the ten years since the high school's inception. I doubt I will have to worry about having my face permanently memorialized on these walls.

The posting of the list is exciting for several reasons. First and foremost, in case there was any doubt, the list confirms I have indeed been admitted to grade 9. I'm not sure what the alternative would be, since I've already been to the grade 8 graduation dance, which should imply I've gotten that ticket punched. Is it possible someone has found out I have only a hazy grasp of the relationship between the area of a parallelogram and the area of a trapezoid? I guess not, because there I am on the list. In home-room 9E with a bunch of kids I've never heard of.

In grade 9 we get to pick an elective subject. One class where we can do our own thing and colour slightly outside the lines of the mandatory curriculum. But not so far outside the lines that anyone would notice and haul you back in. I picked my elective way back in June. I chose typing. I don't remember what the other choices were besides Latin. Probably astrophysics, geoarchaeology, polymer chemistry, and rocket science. All equally unappealing to me. The moto of the high school is "Rere Ratione," which means "think with reason." Underneath the moto, there's a crest that has a geometry set, including a compass, triangle and protractor, on the left-hand side, and the obligatory stylized nuclear symbol on the right. There is clearly no room for other pursuits in this universe.

Our home-rooms are grouped by elective. Latin aficionados are in 9A. The science types are somewhere down the alphabet from there. Typing and machine shop are in 9E. I have no idea what the kids in 9F are taking, but the naming protocol for the sections isn't even trying to be subliminal. It's more than clear to me that Latin will land your portrait on the wall in the hall outside the principal's office in perpetuity, while typing won't even result in a grade that registers on the marking scheme.

* * *

All kinds of kids show up in grade 9 we've never seen before, including the Catholic kids who have their own school that goes up to grade 8. When the Catholic kids on our street started kindergarten, they disappeared into a parallel universe, moving in and out of their houses like water molecules across a permeable membrane. There, not there. There, then not there again. They don't emerge until high school, at which point the rest of us have forgotten who they are. Other new kids get bussed in from Chalk River just to the east and from as far west as Deux Rivieres, forty-five miles up the river. There are three streams in high school: five-year academic, four-year technical and three-year occupational. The kids from up and down the Valley are tech-ers or occ-ers. The boys wear baggy farmer jeans with the tail of their rat-tail comb sticking out of the back pocket, and the girls wear aggressively blue eyeshadow below their teased hair.

In 1969, the (male) employees of CRNL earned an average of $80,000 in today's dollars. In contrast, the average (male) income in Renfrew County in today's dollars is $63,000. Compared to the Ottawa Valley at large, the citizens of Deep River had forty percent more spending power (if we only had something to spend it on). So, there was that. In Renfrew County today, only fourteen percent of the population has a university degree, which is half as many as the country at large. It's not too far a stretch to presume the percentage of university graduates was much smaller in 1969. In the 1958 version of Deep River, there were two hundred PhDs, or one living in every five of the one thousand households in town. In comparison, PhDs in the general population didn't even reach the one percent mark. So, there was that too.

What we had was a classic case of town versus gown. Only upside down. Schisms between locals that live in university towns and the academics that infiltrate them have been traced back as far as twelfth-century Europe. The university students back in that day flocked to France, Germany, Spain and Portugal from a wide array of other European countries to pursue their education, and brought with them their peculiar manners and dress. Latin was the common language for academic pursuits, so the "gownies" didn't understand local languages and dialects, and didn't pretend to try. The Ottawa Valley "townies" that came to Deep River from far and wide for secondary school academic pursuits brought their peculiar dialects and dress to our gowned enclave. And we didn't pretend to understand them either.

But strangely, the two solitudes existed mostly without incident. Or at least, without any incident I ever witnessed. It could have turned into a Jets versus Sharks (with us gowners filling in as the white-bread Jets, and the out-of-towners as the immigrant Sharks) bloodbath, taking its script from the text *West Side Story*, which the four-year kids got to read in English. It actually played out more like *Henry IV, Part 2*, which we were saddled with in the five-year English stream. The plot goes something like this. Prince Hal, heir to the throne, makes fun of the commoners but, in defiance of his father, is misspending his youth by carousing with them in local taverns, and probably drag racing with the family coach-and-four. He knows eventually he'll have to smarten up and "throw off his loose behaviour." He's going to be King Henry the Fifth, after all, and there will be no time for frivolity below his station when that happens. But for now, he can leave his crown in cold storage. And in typing class, at least, we royals can hang out with the street gangs to no ill effect.

* * *

Our typing teacher is Mr. Wilson. Mr. Wilson is older than my dad. He wears a silly bow tie and a vest underneath his suit jacket, just like my grandpa. I don't know how he could have learned to type because usually only girls take typing, except for the three boys in our home-room who are also taking typing. Maybe you don't need to know stuff to teach it. I file this away for future reference. Math teacher may not be off my potential job list after all. The typing room is on the second floor, sufficiently far away from the Latin scholars so that we won't disturb their verb declensions with the ding of our carriage returns. There's a row of grey metal desks with a little drawer in the front to store spare steno pads and a ledge that folds up on the right-hand side so there's a place for your steno pad. The boys don't come to class with steno pads. Unlike the chairs in the regular classroom, the typing room chairs also have casters, so you can roll them in and out from the desk. If you roll the chair too close to the desk, you bang your knees on the drawer handle and snag your stockings on the rolled metal edge. The only sensible posture for typing is to lean forward and hunch, knees safely unmolested. Just like in a real office, Mr. Wilson says. The boys really like these chairs, especially because if you twirl around in them really fast, counterclockwise, the chair goes up really high and sometimes the seat detaches from the rest of the chair. Mr. Wilson does not pay any attention to this, or to the boys in general.

The typewriters are hulks of black metal that could probably make the trip to the moon and back without discernable wear and tear. The keys that take at least thirty pounds of pressure to move them within striking distance of the paper. I notice there are no letters on the keys. Maybe I should have chosen Latin instead. "Okay, girls. Enough with the prattle. We are businesslike in this room. It will help your career to remember that your boss will not like silly girls chattering when there's work to be done," says Mr. Wilson. "We are learning touch-typing here. You won't get far if you can't touch-type. Otherwise, how will you read your shorthand and type at the same time?" In the front of the room over the blackboard, instead of a giant slide rule, there's a topographic map of the typewriter keyboard with all the letters and symbols in the right place. "This chart will be your guide for the first few weeks, but after that, you'll be on your own. Today we'll start learning the home row," says Mr. Wilson.

The home row is where your fingers live. They are not allowed to leave home unless they are temporarily venturing up or down the keyboard. I'm surprised to learn the letters on the keyboard shown on Mr. Wilson's blackboard billboard are not arranged like the alphabet. Instead, they are laid out in what looks like a bad allotment of Scrabble tiles. What word could you possibly make from D, F, G, H, J and K? Latin is looking better by the minute. "F, space, F, F, space, J, space, J, J, space." Mr. Wilson leads us all in collective home-rowing across the page, as he waves his hands like a typewriter chorus conductor. So far so good.

Unlike for home ec sewing, speed is a virtue in Mr. Wilson's typing classroom. We do speed drills every Friday, with Mr. Wilson's trigger finger on the stopwatch. My typewriter seems to have its own built-in speed limit, though. When I go too fast, the keys pile on to each other like football players and I have to pry them apart and start over, leaving my hands looking like I've had a fatal incident with a squid, courtesy of the black ribbon ink. "The quick brown fox jumps over the lazy dog," says Mr. Wilson. "Smile girls! Turn that frown upside down! Whistle while you work! No boss wants to see you unhappy. It's only typing. How hard can it be?" This further cements my belief that Mr. Wilson's hands have never been sullied by a typewriter keyboard, let alone a typewriter ribbon. No wonder not many boys take this class. Rocket science is probably not rocket science compared to a class where the objective is to type invisible letters.

At the end of the speed drill, I release the paper guide and grab the top of the yellow foolscap we use for practice, yanking it up and out in what I hope is a dramatic and highly professional manner, just before it tears right down the middle. "Girls, hand your paper to your neighbour and she'll mark how many words you typed correctly," says Mr. Wilson. He doesn't even have to mark our stuff! I pass my mangled sheet to Marsha on my left.

In between the words that look like they could only have been fashioned by berserkly allotted Scrabble tiles, I have managed to type forty flawless words per minute. Turns out I'm a typing prodigy. My fingers have a magic mind of their own, and I spend a record twenty-two weeks at the top of Mr. Wilson's speed leader board. All the boys drop out of typing before the end of term and migrate to machine shop class. In 1969, senior typists made $1.70 per hour and machine shop workers made $2.59 per hour. The boys clearly knew how to do the math.

In 1901, ninety-five percent of women in the workforce were employed as domestic servants, factory workers (especially in the garment industry, making clothes for other women), primary school teachers (things related to children being squarely in their wheelhouse by default), secretaries or nurses. Their work to bring home all or part of the household bacon paid half of what men were paid.

Moving ahead to 1961, we find that the one-third of adult women who work outside the home were employed as domestic servants, factory workers (especially in the garment industry, making clothes for other women), primary school teachers (things related to children still sitting squarely in their wheelhouse), secretaries or nurses. The good news was that they were now paid fifty-nine cents for every dollar earned by a man. It had taken a mere sixty years for women to creep up to earning sixty percent of what's doled out to the rest of the workforce.

None of us in Mr. Wilson's classroom could have imagined that about ten years hence, typing will have evolved into keyboarding and keyboarding will become socially acceptable to men, as long as they are only seen hunting and pecking at letters with their index fingers, although this is relatively easy because there are letters on the keys. But I'm pretty sure I could have imagined that Latin was never going to resurrect itself as a conversational language. And I'm also guessing, as my fingers fly across my laptop keyboard at 120 words per minute, that the former Latin scholars of 9A no longer remember how to ask Caesar for directions to the vomitorium.

14

Cold Knee War

Mrs. Patterson takes home-room attendance, we mouth the words to "O Canada" as it plays on the loudspeaker, and we half-listen to the principal's announcements in case there's a pep rally or something else that will get us out of school early. But wait a minute. What's this?

"It has come to my attention that some girls are conducting themselves in a less than ladylike fashion. We have rules for a reason and I'm putting you on warning that anyone caught showing up at school in pants will be sent home to change and get five days detention. This is no laughing matter," says Mr. Moffatt. I look to my left at Ian wearing jeans and a Che Guevara t-shirt and look to my right at Malcolm wearing jeans and a Malcolm X t-shirt. I guess Mr. Moffatt doesn't mean the boys.

* * *

By 1970, the Vietnam War had been churning along for fifteen years, with the evil communist faction of the Soviet Union and China cheering on the Godless North, and the God-is-on-our-side United States supplying buckets of cash and buckets of dead bodies to South Vietnam. The hippie pro-peace culture was in high swing, rallying against the futility of trying to solve the two Vietnams' differences. The classic Cold War adversaries were continuing their arsenal envy, but France and China also had their own nuclear weapons, so there was lots of potential planetary annihilation to go around. In 1970, the Doomsday Clock sat at ten minutes to midnight. Tick, tock.

If you recall, Atomic Energy of Canada's mandate was peaceful utilization of nuclear technology. Anti-nuclear sentiment had no purchase in our physics-for-good-not-evil utopia. My dad and his peers poo-pooed the no-nukes protestors that showed up on the TV news (never, ever live and in person in our town), because their lack of atomic enthusiasm extended beyond weapons to nuclear power. "They can't even pronounce the word," my dad sputters. "Nuke-U-ler, they say. What kooks."

Protests in the late 1960s and early 1970s were ubiquitous, because there certainly was a lot to protest. In particular, 1968 was a lynchpin. The American civil rights movement was at its peak, as was the opposition to the Vietnam War. India and Pakistan were bickering via gunfire. Northern Ireland wanted Britain to back off and leave it alone, showing its extreme displeasure via Molotov cocktails. Israel and Palestine were trading missiles across the Gaza Strip, unwilling to cede even a few grains of parched desert. The environmental movement was in full *Silent Spring* swing. Martin Luther King Junior was assassinated. The anti-nuclear movement was digging in its heels. And on and on and on.

The late 1960s spawned many protest methods, most of which shared the suffix "in." The sit-in is pretty much self-explanatory. You sit. The key, though, is to sit *en masse* in a place where a bunch of people sitting down is inconvenient to someone or something. Like in front of a tank. A die-in is not something that would happen if sitting *en masse* in front of a tank goes awry. A die-in is similar to a sit-in, but you lie down on the ground instead of sit down on the ground. A particularly fancy die-in will include drawing chalk lines around the bodies on the ground. A love-in is also similar to a sit-in, except it ups the flower quotient and has music in addition to chants and speeches. If none of these methods appeals, the protest can take the "strike" route. A strike is exactly that: you stop doing something that most people think you ought to keep doing. You can have a hunger strike, a tuition strike, an income tax strike, a voting strike, a fossil fuel strike. Or even a skirt strike.

* * *

The rule is that when you have a locker, you must have a lock, despite the fact that nobody has ever been known to steal chemistry textbooks or swipe *Tiger Beat* pull-outs of David Cassidy. On the other hand, it does provide job security for the dope dealers, because nobody can lift their stash without code-breaking the lock. When you have a lock, you must have a combination lock. A combination lock has three numbers. Not only do I need to remember three numbers, I need to remember the sequence of the numbers and how many times I need to move the dial backwards and forwards, stopping at the numbers I can't remember. My solution for this is to leave the lock almost but not quite latched, so it looks like it's secured but it can be opened just by swiveling the lock part. A brilliant solution, to be sure.

The fashion police have dictated that this year, winter boots must be the kind that lace all the way up the front on metal hooks, pretty much like skate laces. Twiggy wears them even though she doesn't even live in a place that has proper winter. In early November, as soon as I can justify needing to wear winter boots, I proudly flaunt my fashion conformance, strutting my way to school, with the fall sleet congealing on my boot laces and frosting the grommets and hooks. My boots go almost to my knees, leaving the official miniskirt distance of leg open to the slush and wind. By the time I get to school, I can barely bend my legs.

I put on my best enigmatic Twiggy smile, as I Frankenstein my way down the corridor to my locker, giving a jaunty wave to Mrs. Barclay, the secretary who sits at the front of the principal's office. She surely must be impressed by my stylish footwear. I reach out to undo my lock only to discover some helpful idiot has locked my lock. I rack my brain for the combination. Is it 35, 15, 42? Or 15, 42, 35? Or maybe 42, 35, 15? Finally, 35, 42, 15 unlocks it. Fortunately, that's wasted enough time for my laces to transform from frozen black licorice to al dente black linguine. I stuff my coat onto the hook at the back of the locker and consult the timetable that's taped on the back of the door just below the crotch of David Cassidy's red velvet pants. Physics is first period and I'm also about to be late for home-room. And I still have my boots on.

Unlacing my boots presents a logistical problem I have not anticipated. I need to bend down to unlace them except that bending down hikes my skirt up to maximum pettipant. Mrs. Barclay raps on the window of the office. "Not very ladylike," she says. Well what else am I supposed to do? I turn around, spy the stack of science and math textbooks that never leave my locker, and quickly figure out they have better and more practical things to do. I squeeze my butt into the locker and sit on the books to wrangle with my boot laces. I'm stuck with this boot choice for the rest of the winter. I whined my way into them and am loathe to whine my way out. Suddenly, brown galoshes with my shoes already in them don't seem like such a bad idea.

Home-room. Monday morning. Susan, who sits in front of me, pretends she has an itchy back and slinks her right hand behind her to wave a note in my direction. I nonchalantly drop my pencil off the front of my desk so I can snag the note when I lean down to pick up my pencil. "Noon in the girls' gym," it says. Except it doesn't have the possessive apostrophe. We're in grade 10. "Girls only. Secret meeting. Pass it on." After I've read it, I reach back and drop it on to Nancy's desk while pretending to yawn. The note makes its way around the classroom, preceded by many studied and perfected motions of note-passing subterfuge. I'm not completely sure what this is about, but I'm guessing it has something to do with the pants thing. There was an article in the school paper this week about the new decade and how it's time to leave the '60s behind, including the dress code for girls. Mr. Moffatt doesn't know who wrote it because all it says is "by Girls with Cold Knees." I thought that was pretty funny. Mr. Moffatt, I guess not so much.

* * *

Bras were only ever apocryphally burned in public in the 1960s, but clothing and expectations of "beauty" have been proxies for female oppression ever since women started taking up the cause of emancipation. In 1968, a bunch of women's rights advocates demonstrated at the Miss America contest, an act of disobedience that involved flinging perceived symbols of female disempowerment, including girdles, nylons, hairspray, bras, makeup, high heels, and false eye lashes, into garbage cans on the boardwalk outside the Atlantic City hotel hosting the festivities. Apparently, the plan to burn the contents of the cans was scuttled when the police did not provide a permit because the boardwalk was made of wood and presented a fire hazard. Being law abiding citizens, the protesters settled for unfurling banners and chanting "No more Miss America." Debra Barnes Snodgrass, the incumbent Miss America, took exception to this. In her view, these renegade women were diminishing the accomplishments of beauty pageant contestants in perfecting their appearance and honing their talents in baton twirling, tap dancing and juggling so they could attain scholarships to earn diplomas in early child education or attend secretarial school, prior to moving on to solving world hunger.

Meanwhile, some women in the U.S. were working hard to get an Equal Rights Amendment in front of Congress to eliminate employment and other discrimination on the basis of gender. Betty Friedan and others did manage to get Congress to pass the amendment in 1972, but they could not get it ratified by the requisite three-quarter majority of states. You might think this was due to men standing in the way. You would be only partly right. Phyllis Schlafly, a constitutional lawyer from Missouri, was the powerhouse behind the Stop ERA movement, arguing that the provisions of the ERA would make women less safe and more economically vulnerable. She began each of her stump speeches by thanking God and her husband for letting her speak on behalf of the interests of all women and the preservation of the family. So here we have it. Two of many instances where women were their own worst enemy in their struggle to become equal members of society.

* * *

When the lunch bell rings, I join a stream of girls heading towards the gym. Instead of the usual chatter we're strangely silent, as if being quiet will deflect attention from the fact that something is definitely up. The girls' gym is filling up fast. Linda stands watch at the door for teachers. There's a buzz of anticipation. I sit on the floor beside Susan, while the girls who write the school paper go up on the stage at the front of the gym. "It's 1970," says Carol. "And we are stuck in our mother's world! Who wants to have to wear girdles? Why shouldn't we be able to wear what we want to wear? If Mr. Moffatt wants to give us five detentions, we'll show him five detentions! This is how it's gonna to go down. Starting today, we're going to hold a sit-in outside the principal's office. Tomorrow, I'm asking every single one of you to come to school in pants. And we'll keep wearing pants every day until they tear up the dress code that makes us dress in dresses. Bring your pants with you in the morning, in case your mother doesn't let you out of the house wearing them. We can change in the girl's change room. We have the power, Mackenzie girls! What do we want? Warm knees. When do we want them? Now!"

I don't even own any pants, other than snow pants, but I'm guessing I'm probably the same size as my little brother. The next morning, while my mother's fussing about with breakfast, I quickly nab a pair of my brother's jeans out of the laundry basket. I hope he wasn't playing tag in them, although grass stains would at least go with my pettipants. "Gotta go, emergency choir practice," I mumble, as I scam my way out of the house even before the porridge has made its appearance. When I get to school, the gym change room is so full it's wedged shut from the inside. Looks like I'm not alone, anyhow. I decide to head to my locker to make the switch to pants. How could this be worse than any other day struggling in or out of clothes? I uncrumple the jeans from my book bag and determine what I should do is just pull them up underneath my clothes. I unzip my skirt, throw it into my locker, and become an official pants-in rebel. Except I don't think boys wear stockings, garter belts and pettipants under their jeans.

The girls from the newspaper sit on the floor in front of the principal's office door. Silently. Letting their pants speak for themselves. The rest of us go about our day, moving from class to class, avoiding the Twiggy-in-the-headlight glances of the girls who decided not to join in. "What's wrong with dresses? I like wearing my new minidress," Ellen says.

I am so excited to be part of a real protest that I forget to put my skirt back on for the way home. Oops. But at least I have warm knees. When I open the front door to the house, bridge club is still in full swing. "I bid seven no trump," says Mrs. Ross. "Oh, are the kids home from school? I guess we should just go another few rounds. I need to put a pot roast in."

I skulk past the ladies at the card table. As long as they don't look up from their cards, I'm good. "Hi, Mrs. Ross, hi, Mrs. Voss, hi, Mrs. Joyce. Gotta get to my homework!" I slink off to my room, shut the door, kick off my brother's jeans, shove them under my bed and take a deep breath. I'm going to need to figure out how to buy some pants.

I wear my brother's jeans for the rest of the week. Every day, thirty girls sit in the hall outside the principal's office. Every day, more girls show up with their legs wantonly encased in fabric of various kinds. Blue denim, pink crimplene, red plaid polyester, green striped cotton. In Friday's health class, when Mrs. Walker finishes discussing the importance of wearing deodorant, she puts on her reading glasses and picks up a piece of paper from her desk. "We have something important to discuss girls," she says. "This is a memo from Mr. Moffat. He says you are now allowed to wear pants. Tasteful pantsuits or dress pants with nice blouses. Absolutely no denim and no t-shirts. Do not let this go to your heads. If you abuse the rules there will be consequences. You are dismissed."

We look at each other in disbelief. Tasteful pantsuits? Seriously? The war is clearly not over yet. As Churchill said, it's not the end. It's not the beginning of the end. But it's the end of the beginning.

15

Doing the Math

I have a difficult relationship with math. Or more correctly, I prefer to have no relationship at all with math. If it was today, math would be an online date I get roped into, meeting at a coffee shop even though I don't drink coffee. I arrange a friend's fake emergency phone call to rescue me. The phone call never comes. Or that's not true. The phone call, when it comes, is from Mr. Smith from the Mackenzie High School Guidance Department. It's 1971. I have successfully flunked grade 10 math.

In some circumstances this may not be a huge issue. Or maybe in any circumstance that doesn't involve living in Deep River, a place that pretty much invented science, technology, engineering and especially math. If the STEM God doesn't live here, certainly the STEM godfather does. So failing math is a big hairy deal with consequences as dire as a bull in a science lab full of beakers. And a sure path to acceptance at hairdressing school.

The chairs in the math classroom are made for stacking not sitting, although they work pretty well for squirming and slouching. The rubber feet on the bottom of the legs stick to the linoleum and make a fart sound if you move the chair a certain way. The boys do this deliberately and the floor is streaked with black chair trails like dead comets fallen to earth. My spot is the back corner of the back row, just out of range of the chalk dust and just out of the teacher's peripheral vision. Or at least I hope it's sufficiently out of sight, because I tilt my chair back on the cinderblock and use gravity to hang weightless enough for a good nap.

Louis sits beside me, splitting his time between looking out the window at the quadrangle and launching spit balls at the girls in the middle row. There is nothing going on in the quadrangle. There is never anything going on in the quadrangle because no one is allowed to go into the quadrangle. It's probably a secret portal to a land without math. Or at least a land without high school. But the quadrangle, with its dead grass and barren concrete perimeter, is marginally more interesting than the classroom, where everyone except us is huddled over their math notebooks. The consensus seems to be that blue notebooks are for math. My blue scribbler is as fresh as the day after Labour Day even though it's already late enough in the autumn that the sun is well into its the western journey by mid-afternoon.

Louis passes me a folded-up square of paper. He has fashioned it very precisely into a fortune, where you put your thumbs and forefingers into the folds and open it up like a flower to see what's inside. It is not the answer to the question on the board. It is a hangman game with room for four letters. We pass it silently back and forth all the way through the behaviour of polynomials sermon, while the hands of the IBM clock add up the minutes. This is a great way to improve our vocabulary and spelling but does nothing for our math knowledge. Louis's attention span is definitely at odds with wrangling quadratic equations and solving for the intersection of a line. In my opinion, lines can figure out for themselves how, when and where to intersect. This is clearly none of my business.

* * *

Mr. Smith lives around the corner from us. He is famous for watering his front lawn wearing only a black Speedo. He waters his front lawn a lot. I try not to think of this as he tells me I managed to get thirty-five percent in math, which I am guessing is as low as the marking scale goes. Either that or the first thirty-five percent of the marks comes from spelling your name correctly at the top of the page. My options are to repeat the year in the fall or sign up for summer school.

Two months seem much shorter now than it was in the land of childhood. Now, months come and go so fast it seems like a waste of money to buy a calendar, even if it does have an adorable kitten on each new page. But when you are a high school kid, once that final bell rings on June 30, there is an endless stretch of sloth waiting outside the door. By law, this stretch should be filled with sleeping in, hanging out at the beach, eating Popsicles and trying to avoid cutting the lawn. The specter of knuckling down on academics in September isn't even lurking in the shadows. But faced with a choice between six weeks of summer school and spending another entire ten months getting my mandatory-credit ticket properly punched, I was at least smart enough to do the math.

* * *

The Renfrew County School Board presides over 3,000 square miles of scrubby farmland, lakes infested with trout and the occasional dot of humanity ringed with moose-swamps. On a map, Renfrew County looks like a lumpy, tipsy triangle listing to its lower left corner. The right side starts on the outskirts of Ottawa, hugs the shores of the Ottawa River and chugs just past Deep River until running out of hope and steam at Bissett Creek, population 300. If you turn around and head to the bottom, you skirt the northern edges of Algonquin Park until you hit Barry's Bay, population 1,300. As the crow flies it's a mere seventy-five miles from end to end.

The school board has a keen belief in minimizing the consumption of tax dollars and maximizing teacher recreation, so summer school is only offered at one location in the county. The lucky winner this year is Opeongo District High School. In Douglas. Population 600. Which couldn't possibly be farther away from Mackenzie High School. Thankfully, the school board is kind enough to provide a school bus to get us there. But if you know anything about school buses you know they never travel in a straight line.

Deep River is the first pickup point. The bus leaves promptly at seven o'clock in the morning. I am sure that Dante would have to invent a new circle of hell to describe the horror of getting up at the crack of dawn when my peers are getting up at the crack of noon, and then spending two hours on a bus with bad suspension and no air conditioning just to get to a math classroom. We make a leisurely trip on all of the must-see backways and byways of the upper Ottawa Valley, collecting academic delinquents and diligents at random bends in the road. Some kids are weird enough to actually choose to spend their summer getting a jumpstart on next year's installment of physics or algebra.

Our bus tries to fake us out by staying on the main highway for the first ten miles, making fairly good time until it pulls off on the "B" line, a side road to rock-farm country that isn't even road enough to be on a gas station map. The "B" line does not make a beeline. Instead, it follows a vestigial cow path that seems to have been forged by a drunken cow. All of this to pick up a guy at the side of the road wearing an International Harvester cap and a plaid shirt, who in a flash of adolescent brilliance we nickname Freddy the Farmer. He gets on the bus fresh from his morning barn duty. "I bet he's repeating grade 9 typing," I say to my seatmate Dougie, the notion being that flunking math is higher on the academic failure hierarchy than flunking anything else. In reality, he's probably taking grade 13 quantum physics in advance and he's already put in three hours milking cows. All I've done is roll out of bed, pull on some jean shorts and sit on a bus for half an hour. But that thought does not enter my mind. A mixture of dried manure, greasy road gravel, and decomposing roadkill skunk wafts through the windows while my bare thighs weld themselves to the vinyl bench seat. By the time we get there, the bus reeks of melted peanut butter and overripe bananas from our wilted lunch bags.

The school is foreign to me but the classroom is nothing but familiar. I have a pristine blue scribbler. The polynomials are the same. The same IBM clock watches our progress without visible sign of hand movement. The same fog of chalk dust stakes out its regular turf just below the florescent lights. The same complete lack of interest in math.

Luckily, grade 10 math snags a morning time slot. Unluckily, there is also an afternoon session for other subjects in case anyone wants to double up on credits. The bus, of course, does not leave until the brownnosers are finished enriching their high school experience. After consuming my squished, lukewarm ham and cheese sandwich, there isn't much to do but hang around waiting. Maybe I could have used the time for something useful like doing homework but the idea of spending even more time on schoolwork is too much to bear. The weather does nothing to quell the misery. Each day dawns endlessly blue. Each afternoon, the clouds march in, first fluffy and benign then thick, grey and all consuming. By the time the bus belches out of the school yard at three hours past lunch, any hope of tanning hours has evaporated as quickly as sprinkler spray on the parking lot asphalt.

Louis doesn't go to summer school. I think that's because his repeat course load is fuller than a Thanksgiving table. Instead, my new math pal is Anna May. Back in our regular habitat, Anna May and I occupy alternate universes. Anna May hangs out with the smokers and probably knows how to French inhale. Anna May dates. Anna May dates boys who aren't even in high school. Anna May knows how to use an eyelash curler. But the shared shame of math summer school puts us in the same milieu. Or actually, I think I'm the only one who has any relationship with shame. Anna May does not have shame in her lexicon.

* * *

Anna May convinces me that cooling our heels waiting for the return bus milk-run is a waste of summer. We should hitchhike home and enjoy the waning afternoon at the beach. I have never hitchhiked before but luckily Anna May is a pro. She is also an ideal bumming-a-ride asset as she looks exactly like an Anna May should look. The front pocket innards of her cutoff jean shorts flap a good three inches below the scissor line. Her halter top barely contains breasts that are as plump as a baby's bottom. I look about twelve years old, which in hindsight might have attracted an entirely different kind of bad attention. In the manner of teenage girls everywhere, I wear the exact same outfit as Anna May. But in my case, thighs as skinny as clothesline stick out from cutoffs that aren't faded enough for a cool factor and my plunging top flutters in the breeze, hoping one day to harbour secondary sex characteristics.

Anna May is right. Standing on the side of the road getting bombarded with grasshoppers, mosquitos and dust is way better than math study hall. But hitchhiking isn't exactly efficient. Figuring out how many rides it will take to get home and the best places to get dropped off to minimize ride intermissions is like solving a quadratic equation. Something I am still several weeks away from mastering, if at all. We thumb lifts with a series of grizzled truckers with packs of unfiltered Export As rolled up in their sleeves. One from the school to the highway, one to the first town, one to the second town, one to the third town. If we are really lucky, the fourth ride takes us all the way into the centre of Deep River, although that's a bit dicey if we want to avoid calling undue attention to our mode of transportation. Or at least I don't want to call attention. Anna May doesn't bat a single mascara-encrusted eye. Like many things that carry dire warnings from grown-ups, hitchhiking turns out to be pretty much as uneventful and wholesome as a Sunday drive. But I still feel like a swash-buckling renegade, so I learn something more important in summer school than how to solve for x, when y is an independent variable. I learn I can make my own way home from anywhere, which also means I can leave home whenever I want.

Mostly we get dumped off by our ride at Townline Road and make our way on foot down from the highway, our water buffalo sandals sticking to the tar in the seams of the asphalt, while we try to out run the deer flies lusting after our sweaty scalps. We're a scant half hour ahead of the bus, math homework still undone. Only five weeks, three days, nine hours and eleven minutes until summer school is over. Eight weeks, three days, nine hours and eleven minutes until real school begins.

16

Valley Girl

According to linguists that study this stuff, the Ottawa Valley twang developed because of the extreme isolation of the French, Irish and Scottish settlers that ended up in the nether regions of Upper Canada. Scholars also note there are specialized vocabularies in some parts of the Valley and, by the gar, this is true. But Deep River is of the Valley, not in it. The twang was all around us like thick fog, but failed to settle on our enclave, safely and hermetically sealed away from the rest of Renfrew County.

However, being part of the Valley does have its advantages when you are in high school, because it's a long, long way from end to end, and high school culture dictates there must be extramural athletic competition. So extramural competition there will be. Even if it requires at least a sixty-mile bus trip. Even if sixty-mile bus trips require early dismissal for the athletically inclined. I am not athletically inclined, but I am very inclined towards early dismissal. I put all of my brain cells that are not engaged in physics homework, which is to say all of them, to work on getting myself on a team bus. Any bus.

My first course of action is to join the field hockey team because it's the school's first year competing in field hockey and pretty much any girl with a pulse can get on the team. Plus, near as I can tell, field hockey participation is easy to fake as long as I spend an appropriate amount of time running up and down the field in enough proximity to the ball to make it reasonable that contacting the ball with my mallet could happen.

Field hockey does not come with uniforms. Uniforms are for boys and for the girl cheerleaders who cheer for male athletic pursuits. For girl sports, we wear our gym outfits with black or white pinnies over top so we can tell the teams apart. Our gym outfit is a romper jumpsuit in purple with gold buttons (our school colours). Gym rompers are issued in grade 9 and are intended to last the duration of high school. "Make sure you choose a size you can grow into," my mother says. "I'm not planning on buying you another one. And remember how those cotton things shrink!"

There are three boxes full of brand-new gym apparel outside the girls' gym, one each for small, medium and large. All of us grade 9 girls mill about, trying to make the right choice of size. Medium seems to be the most popular: not too small, not too big, just right. As if Goldilocks would be caught dead in gym rompers, even if she was running to escape a bear. I follow the crowd and choose medium. The waist hits me at the hips and the leg openings cover my kneecaps. Room to grow to spare.

Fresh out of the box, the rompers have four vertical darts at the waist, a fabric belt that's attached at the side seams, short sleeves and elastic at the leg openings. The rompers do not stay in this format for long. Like ballet dancers preparing their pointe shoes for service, we must properly doctor the gym outfit before its first official outing. I don't know when this ritual started, but judging by the gym outfits of the grade 13 girls, it's been going on for some time. The specifications for romper modification are handed down by word of mouth, like a secret herbal recipe that will cure cancer. I take my brand-new romper home after school, grab my trusty seam ripper and get to work. I detach the belt from the waist that's not my waist, and rip out the darts so the garment forms a pleasingly shapeless mass from shoulder to leg. The legs need work, though. I rip open the seam that runs around what the romper imagines is the top of my thigh, and pull out the existing elastic, which could easily fit around my hips. I measure two lengths of new elastic around the top of my real thigh, attach it to a tiny gold safety pin, and thread it back through the bottom of the leg openings so the puffed legs will land a little further north of my knees. Ripping the sleeves off is optional, and I decide against it at this point. There's a limit to how much maternal aggravation I want to attract. Voila. Gym attire that conforms to proscribed modifications that will last as long as my gym career.

Our first field hockey game is in Renfrew, sixty-five miles away. We make fun of their valley-speak cheer. "Air Eee Enn Eff Air Eee Dubbya! Go Renfra!" Our team is ultra-cool in our purple sacks, while the Renfrew team wears navy blue rompers with navy buttons, which still have all the darts in them. Our next game is in Arnprior, the maximum distance jackpot, at eighty miles from Deep River. Chemistry gets to bite the dust for this one. Jackpot.

Arnprior's cheer sounds like, "Eh Air Enn Pee Air Aih Ooo Air! Go Errnprrr!" The Arnprior girls all wear navy blue rompers too. Darts intact. Belts, too, even. After a few more away games, it becomes clear that everyone else has blue rompers and we're the only team with doctored purple ones and contrasting buttons. It's like we're aliens recently arrived from Mars who've discovered the strange and backward customs of Earth inhabitants, who are clearly way behind what's hip and happening in outer space.

Our cheer is "Em Eh See Kay Eee Enn Zee Eye Eee," every letter clearly enunciated in our neutral beige Canadian accents, cultural appropriateness marred only by saying zee instead of zed.

By late fall, somehow our rookie team has won all but two of our games, which gets us to the Ottawa Valley field hockey championship. My role in defence is to hang back behind the midfield players, who hang back behind the forwards. I wait in front of our goal line, holding my wooden mallet, which is the width of the business end of a baseball bat cut in half and looks like an elongated "J," with my arms in the classic awkward field hockey stance: left hand halfway down the stick, right hand at the top, right elbow bent at an unnatural angle. Field hockey rules dictate you may only hit the ball with the flat side of the stick and you may not lift your hands above your waist. Another rule I've learned over the course of my field hockey career is that the rounded side of the stick is for bashing your opponent's lower extremities. Unlike real hockey, field hockey does not believe it requires any protective equipment.

I wait and wait, squinting at the action at the far end of the field, watching the clock on the scoreboard counting down the final two minutes of the game. Then suddenly, the crowd around Renfrew's goal pivots and starts stampeding my way, purple rompers trailing a pack of blue ones. One of the blue forwards lines up the white, dimpled ball, which is twice the diameter of a golf ball and three times as hard. She launches a slap shot in the direction of our goal, which is also in the direction of where I'm standing, and the ball hurtles towards my legs. It makes contact just below my knee scabs, adding a new bruise to shins that already look like overripe bananas. The ball rolls back towards the midfield and the final buzzer sounds. I've managed to block the goal. We've won the game and the trophy. Best to go out on a high note, I think. Time to retire my mallet and reclaim my shins.

My friend Angela plays field hockey too, but she has bigger aspirations. "Why don't we try out for cheerleader? We'll get to go on the bus twice as many times 'cause there's twice as many football games!" she says. "We'll get uniforms and everything!" If you look up "cheerleader" in the dictionary, you will see a photo of someone who does not look remotely like Angela or me. We have dark hair, not blonde, hers so wavy it sits on the top of her head like a hat, mine so straight and fine my ears poke out the sides. We have skinny legs, flat chests and arms like Popeye's before the spinach. This does not deter us in the least.

Cheerleader tryouts happen in June just before school ends, so the squad is lined up before football season starts in September. The football players, on the other hand, don't get picked until after Labour Day, because clearly more preparation is required to cheer on a game than to play it. The cheerleader tryouts involve demonstrating essential cheerleader skills. This includes a cartwheel and the ability to elevate yourself at least one foot off the ground when performing the jumps: the spread eagle, the tuck and the herkie. The herkie is the hardest one. You start with your arms in a "V," then you swing them down as you bend your knees to muster up the momentum to get your legs in the air, right leg pointed straight out, left leg bent behind your butt, both legs parallel to the ground. The herkie has a short shelf life: the ability to properly execute a herkie ends abruptly as soon as you graduate from high school.

Angela and I spend countless hours after school in her backyard perfecting our cartwheels and jumps. My cartwheel is unreliable at best, more demented Ferris wheel than anything an ox would agree to be a party to. Angela's cartwheel is as vertical as a Y-axis every single time, and she can even do a back flip.

Finally, the notice appears in the girls' change room. *Cheerleader tryouts. 4pm. Friday, June 13. In the quadrangle. All welcome!* I can't believe the tryouts are in the quadrangle, because nobody is ever allowed in the quadrangle. But maybe the quadrangle is actually the cheerleaders' secret clubhouse. If all else fails, at least I'll get to set foot in the quadrangle. Too bad about the Friday the 13th thing, though. Angela and I gather at four o'clock, along with thirteen other girls, to show our cheerleading stuff. There are nine spots on the squad, but one of them is for the captain, which seems to be like a hereditary monarchy, because she carries over from year to year until she graduates and a new one is crowned. It turns out I'm a little mistaken on that count. It's more like a role for Fidel Castro than Queen Elizabeth. Brenda is the current incumbent, and she presides over the tryouts wearing full cheerleading regalia while the rest of us show up in our baggy purple rompers, looking more like toddlers with saggy diapers than glamourous lust objects. "All right, ladies," Brenda says. "Line up single file at the end of the quadrangle and let's see what you've got. Cartwheels first, then we'll do the jumps. I want to see three cartwheels in a row."

I have never actually done three cartwheels in a row. I've barely ever done one in a row. Maybe if I position myself somewhere in the middle of the pack Brenda won't notice me as much. I move forward in line, lift my arms over my head, close my eyes and go for it. My first cartwheel goes fine. My second one collapses halfway through and on the third one, my right palm lands in a divot in the grass, and I wipe out completely. I'm guessing my cartwheel score is about fifty percent. Better than my math score, anyhow.

Meanwhile, Angela, with her perfect cartwheel form, hits a divot every time and completely fouls out. As long as at least one person is worse than me there's still hope. Brenda runs us through the jumps, makes copious notes in her official cheerleader captain notebook, and tells us the list of successful cheerleaders will go up on the bulletin board outside the principal's office on Monday morning. "If you get chosen for the squad," Brenda says, "you must come to every practice, comport yourself so you do not compromise the integrity of your fellow cheerleaders, and wear your uniform to school every Friday in case there's a pep rally. And if for some reason you do not date a football player, I expect a full explanation."

On Monday, Angela and I hurry to school and crowd around the bulletin board with the other hopefuls. There I am on the list. Second from the bottom. As the first of two substitutes. As in, should one of the chosen few be unable to attend a given football game, the first runner-up will be called to duty. Angela doesn't make either the regular squad or the substitute list. "Oh well," she says, "I have another idea. I'm going to be the manager of the senior volleyball team. You should manage the junior team and then we can travel the bus together." Oh no. Not only do I have to attend cheerleading practice every Wednesday and Saturday, even though I'm not really a real cheerleader, and pretend I know how football works, now I'm also going to have to pretend to know how volleyball works, just because Angela didn't get to be a cheerleader.

As a lowly substitute, I am not issued my own cheerleading uniform. The outfit I don't have is a short purple kilt, gold bloomers that go under the kilt and a gold sweater with two purple stripes down the left side. I borrow the uniform of whomever I'm substituting for, which is never anyone who remotely approximates my size. There are nine cheerleaders. The reason there are nine cheerleaders is that Mackenzie has nine letters. Each cheerleader has one of those letters on the back of her bloomers. It's one of Brenda's important captain duties to decide when we get to reveal the secret under out kilts.

"Rackem, rickem, rockem, ruckem. Get that ball and really fight!" The Cobden cheerleaders yell, right after kickoff. Most of those aren't even real words, I think to myself.

Our squad huddles to figure out our countermove. "Okay, ladies," Brenda instructs. "We'll do 'Themistocles' with a star jump at the end, then flip the skirts. That'll show them Mackenzie High means business!"

We leap into action. "Themistocles, Thucydides, the Peloponnesian War, X-squared, Y-squared, H_2SO_4. French verbs, Latin verbs, sock 'em in the eye. A rick-a-rack, a click-a-clack, a yea Mackenzie High!" We land our jumps, turn our backs to the bleachers and Brenda begins the grand reveal, starting with the M on her butt, as we produce a wave of letters one by one until nine rear ends spell Mackenzie. I'm sure Dr. C. J. Mackenzie, first president of Atomic Energy of Canada, first president of the Atomic Energy Control Board and president of the National Research Council would have been suitably proud.

17

Adventures in Recreation

Recreation was serious business in Deep River. It was treated with the same amount of studious diligence as splitting atoms. Leisure had nothing leisurely about it. There was a recreation director, who oversaw a full-time staff of twelve and a budget of almost $900,000 in today's currency, with the mandate of making the town so much fun nobody would ever want to leave. In other words, kind of creepy.

Fifteen years after Mr. Bland completed his grand pseudo-suburban plan, the town had one thousand households comprised, on average, of two adults (one male and one female) and 2.3 children. There were twenty buildings scattered near the town centre devoted to housing indoor recreation facilities, like an arena and bowling alley, plus space for the more than seventy special interest clubs ranging from the sublime (ballet, barbershop chorus, drama league, wine tasting) to the ridiculous (snail watching, matchbox crafts, conversational Esperanto). There were no less than seven official orchestras, and probably some garage-band orchestras as well.

Mr. Evraire is the person responsible for making sure everyone is sufficiently recreated. Mr. Evraire does his rounds around town in his athletic wear, long before sweatpants were considered clothing with a life outside the gym, overseeing the playing fields, gym sports and swimming lessons. His whistle is always at the ready, on a lanyard around his neck, in case anyone needs an emergency referee. And indeed, a delicate dance is required to ensure the cricket club, rugger club, soccer club, field hockey club and lacrosse club get equal dibs on the available turf. Mr. Evraire's physical fitness facilitators lurk in the parks like secret police, waiting to pounce on idleness and drag it to the baseball diamond. Even the optional activities are mandatory. On any given day, ninety-five percent of the town's inhabitants who are not still in diapers are engaged in some form of cerebral or physical extracurricular activity. By 1970, the sprung wood floor of the gym had already been replaced four times, courtesy of the thousands of enthusiastic pairs of feet that had trodden its boards in the previous ten years.

In the summer of 1972, I'm too old to crash about in the bush and too old to get away with reading books at the beach all summer. I'm already fifteen, for crying out loud. I need a summer job. Or at least that's what my mother says. And that's how I come to be one of Mr. Evraire's summer minions. I am hired as a playground leader at Cedar Park, along with my friend Liz. We each get two official Town of Deep River t-shirts, white with a blue town crest on the left chest. The town crest has a beaver lounging on top of a shield that's bisected diagonally by a river, with an atomic symbol in the upper right quadrant and a white pine in the lower left. You can tell it's a white pine, even though it's blue because of the Group of Seven silhouette. The t-shirt is very fancy and official. It comes in one size, large, and it completely covers my jean shorts. Liz teaches me how to roll it up and knot it so I don't look like quite as much of a dork. Liz's mother is an artist and doesn't even curl or play bridge, so Liz knows a thing or two about being bohemian. We also get whistles and the key to the storage shed at the park that holds all the equipment deemed necessary for recreating. What we don't get is any instruction on exactly what we're supposed to be doing with thirty kids every weekday between nine and noon for the next six weeks. Liz says, "I'm guessing there should be baseball and crafts. But I'm not sure. It's been six years since we've been at summer playground. Why don't you look after the baseball and I'll lead the crafts?" Right. Baseball. That doesn't sound so bad. Baseball pretty much takes care of itself.

The kids start arriving on their bikes just after nine. There's no sign-up for summer playground, it's just show-up. I have no list of which kids to expect and no way to know if who is supposed to be there is there or not there. The only non-negotiable is ending the morning in time to send the kids home for lunch before swimming lessons, unless they've brought their lunch and are going directly to the beach. Either way, where they go after playground and whether or not they get there is none of my business. My role is simply to wrap up the activities by noon, close up the supply shed, and call it a day.

The supply shed is made from corrugated metal with a wooden door held closed with a padlock, in case someone is tempted to walk away with the softballs, Frisbees, yellow pylons and art supplies. "Look," Liz says, "streamers, paper plates, glue sticks and magic markers! This will definitely do! Now I remember how crafts worked." There's also a small picnic table in the middle of the shed covered in boxes of plastic cups and cutlery. I hope we aren't supposed to be feeding these kids. But who knows?

The kids are milling about expectantly. I hope most of them have never been to summer playground before, or have completely forgotten what happens at the playground, or maybe think the playground experience has been completely transformed since last year. Fingers crossed. I don't want to get fired from my first job. I start getting the baseball underway, while Liz sets up for crafts. The baseball diamond is at the far end of the park, near the creek. The grass in the park is more clover than grass, and what little grass that's left is dry and brown even though it's only early summer. The park is watered only from the heavens, and they've been stingy so far this year. With every step I take towards the diamond, dozens of grasshoppers change location. The kids straggle behind me, dragging bats and a bag full of balls and mitts. Baseball is probably not what they had in mind, and even if they did, the diamond would quickly put a damper on things. The diamond has seen better days. At least I hope it has, because it couldn't get much worse. There's a droopy chain link backstop, the baselines are delineated by dried mud, and there are no bases, just vaguely round, two-inch depressions in the dirt formed by generations of sneaker heels. They fill with water when it rains and belch out clouds of dusty sand when it doesn't.

I get the kids to choose two teams by counting off by ones and twos. "All the ones are on one team and the twos are on the other," I say. "Choose a captain and decide who's playing what position. You need to figure this out yourself because it'll teach you responsibility. Playground isn't just about having fun." I totally make that last part up so I can get away with as little as possible, but maybe because of my official t-shirt and whistle, the kids just get on with sorting things out. "Okay. I'll be back at the picnic tables. I'll call you when it's time for crafts," I say. I walk back to the playground base-camp and join Liz, who's deciding on the craft-du-jour.

Something involving paper plates, streamers and glue sticks. I can see she has things under control, so I go into the shed, both to get out of the sun and shield myself from Mr. Evraire's prying eyes in case he decides to check on us. I settle in at the picnic table to kill some time reading and crack open *Love Story* even though I already know the ending. This gig is turning out to be worth the eighty-five cents an hour.

Liz and I are mistaken that there's no particular agenda for playground. This becomes apparent next Wednesday when the town weekly newspaper, *The North Renfrew Times*, arrives at my house. On page six, there's a playground event schedule staring me in the face. Next week, apparently, there's a field day. Liz and I arrive at the park early the next morning and assess the damage. "Do you think these kids even read the paper?" Liz asks. "Will they even know there's supposed to be a field day?" I don't think the kids' newspaper reading habits are the issue. I think Mr. Evraire has decreed there's going to be a field day next week, so field day there will be. I'm not giving up my official t-shirt that easily.

Mr. Evraire's designated field day turns out bright and sunny. Liz and I do an equipment inventory. We have pylons. We have plastic spoons. We find practice golf balls hidden away in the shed. We have streamers. We have baseball bats. Okay then. Spoon race with plastic golf balls and plastic spoons. That's got to take a while, what with the east wind and all. Three-legged slalom course with the pylons, kids tethered together with streamers. And the grand finale, a baseball bat relay race around the park, with five teams, a semi-final round and a final. All we need now is prizes. We have no prizes. "Wait, yes we do," says Liz. "First prize, you get to help out with crafts for the week. Second prize you get to be a captain in baseball and borrow the whistle. Third prize, you get to help put the stuff in the shed at the end of the day." Not bad, I think, except for the part where Liz's helpers win first prize and mine win second. But if it all goes well, for the rest of the week we'll have even more time to read. Mr. Evraire does not show up for our field day. Job security for at least a few more days.

On the next weekly paper day, I snatch the *North Renfrew Times* off the coffee table before anyone else gets to it, and open it to page six. Sure enough, Mr. Evraire strikes again. Next week there's supposed to be a breakfast hike. Involving breakfast, I suppose. Liz and I show up early again on Thursday. Maybe this is Mr. Evraire's subversive way of getting extra effort for his eighty-five cents. I think the only way this is going to work is if we get the kids to bring their own breakfast. "Let's tell the kids if they want to go on the hike, they need to bring an egg, two slices of bacon, and two pieces of bread with them Monday morning," I say. I decide the hike destination should be Balmer Bay Beach, about two miles down the dirt road that runs perpendicular to the firebreak. Factoring in the distance from Cedar Park to Balmer Bay Road, it's about three miles one way. Okay. Scrap the hike-hike, it will be a bicycle hike. A bicycle hike, Mr. Evraire! A completely new invention! I'm winning the playground leader of the year award for sure. In fact, I bet they'll invent the award just for me.

Breakfast hike day is once again warm and sunny. I tell the kids to put their breakfast supplies into the blue plastic baskets that hang on the front of every bike, and get on their bikes to follow me to Balmer Bay. I have fire-starting and cooking supplies. Liz has art supplies. Liz has decided art should be part of the breakfast hike. I hope she's not trying to beat me out for playground leader of the year. We head out like a marauding gang of junior Hell's Angels, a pack of blue CCMs spanning the entire width of Hillcrest Street. We merge on to the dirt road towards Balmer Bay Beach, where it becomes clear that dirt roads and raw eggs are not a good combination. "Miss! My egg broke!" "Miss! My egg broke too!" I tell the kids to walk their bikes the rest of the way, and Liz stays behind to encourage the bike walking, while I pedal on ahead to get the cooking fire started. I should have had breakfast before I left. This is quickly turning into a lunch hike.

I boot it by standing up on my pedals, and make it to Balmer Bay in about ten minutes. I gather kindling for the fire, dig a pit in the sand, arrange the wood and light the fire with only twelve matches. A personal best. Liz shows up about half an hour later with most of the kids we started with, all of whom are covered in dust from the dirt road. We tell the kids to find a good stick for their bacon and toast. That should take up some time. "And hand over your eggs," I say, "broken ones too. We're making scrambled." Liz teaches the kids how to thread their bread on the sticks, wrap it with bacon and hold it over the fire. The bacon grease sends up plumes of smoke and the bread gets singed with black. The ultimate sign of a good outdoor meal. The river is still and the only sound over the crackling fire is breakfast being eaten and loons complaining about something. But no one complains about the breakfast.

The weekly paper arrives on schedule. This time I wait until everyone else has read it from stem to stern, before I reluctantly seek out page six. Mr. Evraire has out-done himself this time. Now we are going to have a mid-summer parade and compete with the other three playgrounds in town for best float, with fabulous prizes supplied by the recreation office. Now they cough up the prizes.

On Monday, we tell the kids there's going to be a parade this week. "I already know," says Terry. "My mother told me." Crap, crap and crap. Mr. Evraire probably called all the mothers. The good news is the mothers are guaranteed not to be at the parade. They'll be at the beach. Like usual. The parade thing still kind of has us stumped. Especially the float part. But I am not going to let Mr. Evraire get the better of me. If we can do a bicycle hike, why not a bicycle float? "Boys! When you go home today, get as many hockey cards as you can and we'll attach them to your bike spokes. And wear your Expos baseball hats for the parade. Expos shirts if you have them," I say. Liz gets busy making streamer pompoms to attach to the girls' bike handlebars and paper plate hats with streamers fashioned into roses.

Parade day dawns wet and drizzly. Good news for Cedar Park grass. Bad news for parade day. But there's not much summer left, so the show must go on. I assemble the kids and bikes at the top of the park, while Liz collects the girls' finery out of the shed. "Okay, kids," I say. "When you get there, ride so close together you can touch the person beside you. Girls at the front, boys at the back." The Cedar Park pack heads towards downtown where the parade is set to circumnavigate the town quadrilateral. I notice that Morison Park has created floats out of wagons confiscated from little brothers and sisters, each one a different colour that collectively forms a rainbow. Good theme for today. Hill Park has all the kids decked out in cowboy and Indian costumes, brandishing cap guns, with their dads' axes standing in as tomahawks. Then it really starts to pour. The Cedar Park girls morph into vampires as their streamers melt in the rain, dripping red dye #2 down their faces. The hockey cards on the boys' bikes do not fare much better.

Only two more weeks of playground to go. Give me your best shot, Mr. Evraire. I've got this one.

18

The Art of the Theatre

Mr. Fraser tells us to lie on the floor of the stage and close our eyes. "Relaxing is very important," he says. "You can't be a good actor or actress unless you can control your body." This sounds good to me, earning a high school credit while snoozing, which didn't work so well for me with math. But it looks like theatre arts is the antithesis of math, since relaxing is not only encouraged but mandatory. Mr. Fraser has a fondness for Fraser tartan ties and always wears a pilled cardigan or sweater vest over his white button-down shirt. We call him Bobo, because his receding hairline starts mid scalp, with a shock of wiry red hair that stands straight up like a circus clown.

Theatre arts class shows up as an option in grade 11 and takes place in the main gym, the one with the stage. Everything we do in the class happens on stage or backstage. Some of the backstage activities are sanctioned by Mr. Fraser and some are not, like the dope smoking. But Mr. Fraser doesn't seem to know what dope smells like so the joints get passed without adult interruption. Possibly, dope smoking is an asset for the pursuit of theatre arts, except maybe not when memorizing lines is required. I don't really smoke it anyway, the 1970s version of marijuana being so rife with twigs and other detritus that it's as harsh as bleach when it hits my throat, which cannot be good for my acting voice. This does not deter the boys, who are mostly in theatre arts for the easy credit. Easier than rocket science, anyway. Even though it takes at least a whole joint to elicit a slight buzz, the boys pretend they are as stoned as a rock star on a single puff, eyes half shut, jaws slack. Counts as acting though, I guess.

Theatre arts class is new to me, but the theatre is not. I have been in plays since grade 7, both musical and non-musical. I always try out for the lead. Because I only audition for the main female role, I consistently sabotage my chance of getting any other decent part. Because really, there isn't any other decent part, in my opinion. The good news is I'm always cast as the understudy for the lead. The bad news is this means I usually fill a token bit-part to legitimize my existence in the cast. As an understudy, I need to learn all the lines and cues, memorize the stage blocking, and have an appropriate costume in abeyance, in case the lead is unable to complete her duties on any given night. Unlike on Broadway, where the understudy regularly fills in once or twice a month, the short run of a high school play means the marquee actress is extremely committed to the concept that the "show must go on," so I never do.

Our theatre arts play this year is *The Octogenarian.* Mr. Fraser gets to choose the play. Mr. Fraser also teaches English so he thinks he's the authority on plays. It could be worse. He could have chosen Shakespeare, which has hardly any parts for girls. Mr. Fraser tells us even the girl parts were played by boys back in Mr. Shakespeare's day. I'm not sure why he thinks this information is interesting or useful, but I write it down in case it's on the test. What do you put on a theatre arts test anyhow? I guess I'll find out eventually.

Maybe he chose *The Octogenarian* because it doesn't require much in the way of a set or costumes. Just two beds, a wooden ramp, pajamas and leotards. My initial hope that our play might be chock full of juicy roles for girls fizzles quickly. Even though the male/female ratio in theatre arts is skewed towards female, *The Octogenarian* has no female lead nor named female characters. On the upside, there's no lead to audition for so I get to skip the understudy duties this time. "You'll find this very challenging, girls," says Mr. Fraser. "This stuff is about as avant-garde as it gets." Or at least as avant-garde as it could get in 1962, the year the play was written.

The girls get to be a modern-day Greek chorus, decked out in leotards and black tights. Our job consists of making wind sounds, wave sounds and thunder sounds, while perched on a slanted wooden ramp, pretending to be a boat in a storm. We all have leotards, of course. I wear mine to school almost every day as a top with my jeans, despite the inconvenience of having to completely undress when I need to go to the bathroom because the leotard is a single piece of fabric. The implicit fashion decree of the leotard has reached peak adoption, so the line-up for the girls' bathroom now stretches down the hallway. This has not escaped Mr. Moffatt's notice. "It has come to my attention," he says in his morning announcements, "that girls are loitering in the hallway outside the bathroom. I hope none of you are smoking in there! I will be monitoring this situation closely." Sure, Mr. Moffatt. In a few years, the leotard top will go out of style and be replaced by the jumpsuit. Good luck with that, Mr. Moffatt.

Mr. Fraser decides that since we're going to all the trouble of staging our play, what with the extensive work going into sets and costumes, we should enter it in the Eastern Ontario Drama Festival, which is conveniently being held in Deep River this year. I'm okay with that. A festival should be fun. Too bad we don't get to travel out of town, though. That's a bummer. We've been rehearsing the play for about four weeks now. Aside from the girl chorus, the other characters are a boy and an old man in a hospital, and a bunch of other boys who are soldiers. But they're not real soldiers, they're pretend soldiers that live in the old man's imagination. Actually, everything is pretty much in the old man's imagination. Only of course it's not really an old man, it's Robert pretending to be an old man. Despite our weeks of rehearsal, I have no idea what this play is supposed to be about and I don't think anyone else does either. Mr. Fraser says, "It's about the actor's experience of inciting imitative desire and emphatic spontaneity. We'll be accepting that first prize trophy for sure."

The drama festival takes place on the weekend and we're slated for Saturday afternoon. We take to the stage at two o'clock. I, and the rest of the girls in the chorus, whoosh, whistle, murmur, growl, grumble and gurgle our way through our part. Thankfully, unlike what's happened at practically every rehearsal so far, we don't even fall off our slanted platform when we pretend to be a ship, undulating up and down in unison with the invisible waves. The finale is an acapella rendition of "One Tin Soldier." This song has nothing whatsoever to do with the topic of the play. Or at least I don't think it does. Or maybe it does. Who knows? What about that "valley" reference? Is that a hidden clue? We end to a smattering of tepid applause. The people at the jury table sit in stunned silence. Mr. Fraser joins us for the curtain call, smiling broadly.

We don't win first prize or any prize. Apparently, there is no prize for bewildering the judges. "Maybe Shakespeare next year," says Mr. Fraser.

* * *

Each summer, the National Theatre School runs a program for students to perform in a national touring company. You get paid and everything. I decide I will become part of the cast. Becoming part of the cast requires travelling to Ottawa in the spring to audition. The audition requires a Shakespeare soliloquy, a poem recitation and a song. This I can do, I think. Maybe. I don't bother sharing this ambition with anyone, especially not Mr. Fraser, because then someone might point out to me the difficulty of pulling this off or might point out to me that acting is not a thing people do for work. Even summer work. It does not occur to me that I'm compounding the difficulty by preparing on my own, in secret, in my room. At night.

The poem choice is easy. My favourite is *Jabberwocky*. I can even recite it in German. "Es brillig war, die schlichte Toven wirrten und wimmelten in Waben; und aller-mümsige Burggoven die mohmen Räth ausgraben." Should I do it in German? Surely nobody else will be this clever. Or maybe they won't even notice it's German because Jabberwocky isn't exactly in English. The song choice is easy: "I Don't Know How to Love Him," from *Jesus Christ Superstar*. I sing it all the time in my room. For the Shakespeare, I'm thinking *Taming of the Shrew*. I've never read it, but there's got to be at least one good female soliloquy in there.

On the day of the audition, I tell my mother I'm holing up at Debbie and Ruth's house for the day rehearsing for a theatre arts play. I scuttle out of the house just before sunrise and run up to the highway to catch the bus to Ottawa. I spend the two-hour trip reciting my lines in my head and singing under my breath. I walk from the bus station to the National Arts Centre where the audition will take place. I've only ever been to the NAC once, on a field trip last year to see *Godspell*. It only opened in 1969, my first year of high school. It's a huge mass of imposing concrete, interrupted at brief intervals by a façade of crushed granite from the Laurentian Mountains. The windows are narrow slits that look towards the Rideau Canal, which is muddy sludge this time of year. I finally find the door and enter a hallway packed with kids clutching binders and doing vocal warm-ups. "The tip of the tongue, the teeth, the lips, the tip of the tongue, the teeth, the lips, the tip of the tongue, the teeth, the lips..." Was I supposed to have a binder? Does my inside voice practice on the bus count as a vocal warm-up?

"Sign in over here," a woman with a clipboard says. "Print your name and we will call names in order." Maybe I should have camped out overnight. Maybe I should have done a lot of things I didn't do. But I'm here now. I slide down to the floor of the corridor with my back against the wall, pull out *A Wrinkle in Time* and start to read it for the umpteenth time, while the kids around me study their binders. What the heck's in those binders anyhow? I also should have brought a lunch. And maybe a dinner. And maybe a breakfast. And maybe a hope in hell.

After I've almost made it through my book for the umpteenth-plus-one time, the clipboard lady calls my name and ushers me into an audition room on the lower level with an obstructed view of the melting canal. "Hand your sheet music to the pianist, please, and to begin, give us your short bio before we head into the soliloquy." Ummm. Sheet music? Bio? What's a bio?

There are two men and a woman seated at a table, each with piles of paper in front of them and pens in every colour, especially red. They are going to mark me in pen. Is it too late for the escape hatch in the floor to open and swallow me up? "I forgot to bring my sheet music," I say. "But it's *Jesus Christ Superstar*, so maybe you have it already. I'm from Deep River and I'm in grade 11 theatre arts."

"Deep River," the woman says, "that explains a lot."

Really? I dearly hope the reputation of the purple rompers has not proceeded me all the way to Ottawa. I take a deep breath and launch into my best rendition of Katherine's final soliloquy from *Taming of the Shrew*, that is if Katherine's favourite outfit is shapeless Howick overalls and a purple t-shirt, an outfit that I suddenly realize is unwittingly echoing the profile of my gym outfit. "Fie, fie! Unknit that threat'ning unkind brow. And dart not scornful glances from those eyes. To wound thy lord, thy king, thy governor. It blots thy beauty as frosts do bite the meads." I finish my soliloquy flawlessly, as far as I'm concerned. I look towards the table and the faces of the panel are impassive. The red pens are flying.

After a brief pause in the furious writing, the man on the left looks up and says, "Have you ever seen *Taming of the Shrew* performed?"

"No," I say.

"Okay," he says, "I have an idea. We have some time. Can you do your piece again, only this time, pretend as if Katherine has actually been tamed." Okay, he wants to see my range, I think. I redo the drill, but with a healthy dose of shrewish contrition. Nailed it, I bet.

On to the song. The pianist takes his place at the piano and notices the lack of sheet music. Buoyed by my Shakespearian triumph, I tell him my song. The corners of his mouth lift so imperceptibly you'd need a Geiger counter to detect it. He takes a brief look at his watch, positions his fingers on the piano keys and says, "Great, no problem. I've played it forty times already today. Take it away."

After the audition, I have to really boot it the mile-and-a-half to get back to the station in time to catch the last bus of the day. I hope my mother hasn't called Mrs. Dixon in the meantime. But, of course, she would never have called Mrs. Dixon. She doesn't even know Mrs. Dixon. The Ottawa bus station is almost empty. Just an old man with a paper shopping bag that looks like it holds a bottle of something, sitting on one of the pew-like wooden benches. It used to be a train station before it became the bus station, and for some reason all train stations have wooden benches in the waiting room. Nothing in any public transit waiting room is ever designed to facilitate waiting. But fortunately, the westbound Voyageur "coach" is just wheezing into the station when I arrive, ready to forge upstream parallel to the Ottawa River, past Mattawa to North Bay, where it will turn in for the night. I climb aboard and claim a seat behind the driver, which has an ashtray that's only slightly overflowing with butts. It smells like the bathroom at the back has not fared quite as well in the overflowing department.

During my trip back to Deep River, while I look out the window at the shadows that are swallowing up the endless view of rocks and trees, I think about how my illustrious and awesome summer theatre career will unfold. Maybe I'll finally grow boobs. And maybe the National Theatre boys will like me. And at the very least, I'll get out of town. To exotic places like Moosejaw, Saskatoon and Kamloops. Several other time zones, even!

Two weeks later, I get a fat letter in the mail from the National Theatre School. They are delighted to offer me a position. With the northern Ontario version of the touring company. Starting in North Bay. Ending in Thunder Bay. Spending the middle in the middle of nowhere. This is insulting. I rip up the letter and hide it under my bed. I guess I'll be a playground leader for the summer. Again.

19

Turning Pro

When I tried out for *Jeopardy* in the early 2000s, my amusing anecdote for Alex Trebek was that I was a professional figure skater. This is absolutely true.

Figure skating practice is before school, because that's when there is ice at the arena with no hockey players. Figure skating is tolerated, but it is way far from the arena's raison d'être. I get up by myself in the winter morning dark, shrug on my parka and slip out the door with my skate bag, a vinyl tote shaped like an "L" with a zipper up the front. My skating skirt, turtle neck, pullover sweater and gossamer thin tights are intended to balance on the precipice between appropriate warmth and freedom of movement once I get to the rink. In theory. I forge through the ice fog, which is what you get when it's too cold to snow and the water vapour crystalizes into particles that suspend in the air like a mist of diamond fragments that ravage my cheeks with a thousand cuts. The territory between the top of my boots and the bottom of my coat feels like it's made from frozen rubber.

Ten girls dressed exactly like me converge at the arena door. "I hope they didn't forget to unlock it like last time," says Linda. But we're in luck. The door is open. The arena has something that resembles heat in the lobby and change rooms, emanated by radiators that hiss out scalding steam that condenses on the floor. You can sort of warm up if you stand right in front of them, if you want to risk wiping out on the indoor ice puddle. I get to the change room and peel the vinyl handle from my frozen mitt and do a battle to the death with the zipper on my skate bag, which is stuck halfway down. Eventually I liberate my skates, which have yellow plastic skate guards that fit on the bottom of the blade, held on by a metal spring that hooks over the back, because metal and winter is always a good combination.

I have new skates this year, endorsed by Maria Jelinek because Maria's Canadian and, along with her brother, she won the World Pairs Skating Championship, which means she should know a thing or two about skates. I had to send away for the skates by tracing the outline of my feet on a piece of paper and putting it in the mail to Toronto. The skates I get back sort of fit, but no matter, they are exquisite: kid leather with blades that attach with removable screws so you can replace them with new ones when they wear out, or if you need to swap between ice dance blades and pairs skating blades, a requirement I can only aspire to in my wildest dreams. The blades come finally honed with a concave centre for knife-sharp edges that will last until they need to be sharpened, at which point they will be doomed to sharpening by the hockey skate expert who works the arena's sharpening machine. After that, they more closely resemble the hockey skate blades. Hockey is as hockey does.

The ice part of the arena is marginally warmer than the air outside. Early morning is patch time. A patch is a section of ice you have for your own exclusive use to practice figures. It's called figure skating because, well, figures. Figures are the equivalent of scales on the piano. They are practiced ad nauseam and nausea sometimes does ensue. There's a grid map of the arena ice surface on the wall where you claim your patch for the day. Today, I'm lucky to get one in the upper left corner by the boards. That way, I only need to delineate two sides of ice sovereignty. I push off with my left foot and stick the back of my right skate blade parallel to my instep and jam it in the ice to make a line that forms the right and bottom sides of my patch. Then I move to the middle of my personal rink real estate and use the same technique to make a crosshatch that will form the centre of my figure eight. I push off clockwise with my right foot to start an outside edge. I move slowly to do my best to achieve a circular circle. I keep my back foot close to my instep and hope my initial push was strong enough to take me all the way around the top of the eight without running out of steam before I can bring my left foot and right arm forward to provide enough momentum to make it back to centre. That's the theory, anyway. And theory rarely meets practice in my reality.

The thing about the figure part of figure skating is that on test days you have to do three complete tours of each eight, but leave only one visible mark on the ice. If anyone in the history of ice has ever managed this, I would like to bonk her over the head with my skate guard. Even worse, advanced figures involve inserting a little "loop-de-loop" on the top and bottom of the eights, a whimsical segue that seems like it should be fun but is actually a torturous experiment in defying the laws of physics as defined by Mr. Newton. *Objects in motion tend to remain in motion with the same speed and in the same direction, unless acted upon by an unbalanced force.* If that's not torture enough, there are figures where you start out forward and change to backward halfway through the circle. You aren't even supposed to look down at the ice when nonchalantly reversing your quarter-inch steel blade from north to south while being suspended over the ice by a micron of melting water. Who decided this is a good use of my time?! Probably Maria Jelinek, although Maria also says you should wear bare feet in your skates. Clearly, Maria is delusional or has never skated on hockey ice. Or has certainly never lived in a place like Deep River.

Figure skating ice is designed so the skate edges can sink in and grip. Figure skating ice is best at about twenty-two degrees Fahrenheit. Hockey ice is designed so that pucks will move quickly, and "fast" ice happens at about sixteen degrees Fahrenheit. These six degrees of separation may seem small, but only if you aren't wearing skates. That's the other reason we're here at seven in the morning: the ice has to freeze hard enough in time to not muck up hockey practice, which takes place at the more sensible hours of after school and weekend mornings after sunrise. By then, the radiators will have made more of a commitment to a frost-free dressing room interior. Much better for hockey players who wear pads and knitted outerwear and as much as they want under their jerseys. And even socks in their skates. That's okay. My legs tough it out in my regulation figure skating tights under the kilt that ends just short of my crotch. When your legs go numb you don't feel the cold so much anymore.

* * *

I take a bunch of tests and gain a chest full of figure skating badges and medallions, which along with a quarter will get you a bottle of Coke. I like ice dancing because I hate jumps and with ice dancing you don't need to catch any air. Just like normal dancing, ice dancing has set patterns you need to learn. Unlike normal dancing, each standard ice dance can be done only one way to one official song. The Dutch Waltz is the first dance in the preliminary dance series. Preliminary means "before." Before you get to the meaty stuff like the Paso Doble and the Kilian, whatever the heck they are. For the Dutch Waltz, I circumnavigate the rink to "Some Day My Prince Will Come," inside and outside edging my way to the one-two-three, one-two-three. I need to learn how to do it solo and with a partner because the test requires a partner. The partner needs to learn it backwards without looking. There are no boy figure skaters so all of the partner candidates are girls. I do not sign up to be a partner.

The arena plays the official ice dance music via an official record on the official record player in the hockey announcer's booth. It blares out over the state-of-the-art 1966 PA system (although it's already 1972), skipping at will. I listen to "Some Day My Prince Will Come" about twenty times a day, five days a week during November, December, January, February, March and most of April, with no visible sign of any princes.

* * *

I'm doing really well at this skating thing, I think, so I decide to volunteer to do a solo at the next skating recital. Maybe there will be scouts in the audience. Who knows? Nobody else has signed up for a solo. Brilliant, I think. I'll be the star. I choose my music with great care. "In-A-Gadda-Da-Vida." It's got lots of dramatic parts where I can insert jumps. I don't concern myself with the fact the song is seventeen minutes long. I develop my routine during patch time. No time for figures for me. I'm moving the next level. I do this without bothering to involve Kathy, my skating coach. It's none of her business anyhow and besides, I don't want anyone messing with my creativity. There's just one small problem: the jumps. But I'm an actress. Maybe I can make them think there's jumps just by waving my arms in the air. Maybe.

After school before hockey practice starts, I get the guy in the booth to put on my Iron Butterfly record and cue it to my song. I'm really good at the backwards crosscuts that signal you're about to execute a spectacular jump, only in my case it's a bunny hop, the jump where your foot barely leaves the ice and you don't even have to rotate around in the air. But I finish with an impeccable ballet arm flourish.

Skating exhibition day. I have not told anyone I'm a headliner, although my parents are in the stands, thinking it's a run-of-the-mill skating recital and they show up to see if they're getting bang for their figure skating bucks. After the requisite group precision skating number, I return to the ice by myself. Iron Butterfly gets their groove on as I stand centre ice in my average, every day skating attire. Down beat in one. I curtsy to the less–than-crowded arena seating area and push off to the right, starting the crosscuts for my first jump. Maybe it's the extra bright arena lights. Maybe I laced my Maria Jelinek's wrong. But things go completely off the rails from here. I don't land my first bunny jump nor any other jump after that. For seventeen minutes. "Well that didn't go so well," says my mother. "Are you sure those Maria Jelinek's were worth the money?"

* * *

My illustrious skating career is showing signs of stalling. I don't think there is such a thing as solo ice dancing at the

Olympics. But there's another way I can monetize my skating proficiency. I sign up for the skating coach course that's held at the Pembroke arena so I can qualify to teach learn-to-skate and hockey power skating. It's a day-long session that provides us with the pedagogy required to create skating proficient four-year-olds and to teach hockey players how to do an impressive hockey stop. That's the good news. The bad news is when I start to get paid money to do anything skating related, I have to change from amateur to professional figure skating status. This doesn't mean much of anything except I have to pay five times as much to take any further tests. So ironically, being a professional skater permanently halts further skating skill enhancement.

I make $1.60 an hour at my part-time skating teaching job. My learn-to-skate class has a gaggle of four- and five-year-olds wearing snow pants, toques pulled down to their eyebrows and mitts with strings that wind their way through the sleeves of their jackets. They aren't tall enough to cling to the top of the boards and the differential between the weight of their outerwear and the fulcrum of their skate blades makes staying vertical a minor miracle. They are learning to master the new skater shuffle: parallel feet, hip width apart, quarter-inching forward at a speed that would put a snail to sleep. It takes them half the class time just to get to line up at the blue line. Which is fine with me because that means I have more time to figure out what I'm going to do with them.

First up, I think the snowplow stop. Except, you have to actually be moving to accomplish a stop. Maybe I can get them to form the snowplow stop position while semi-standing at mid-ice. "Kids, put the heels of your skates together," I say confidently. "No, the heel is the part of your foot without the toes. Can you make a 'V' with your skates? No, a 'V' looks like the pointy part of a triangle. What's a triangle? Okay, never mind. Let's practice picking up one foot and pushing it forward and then do the other one. Yes, Megan, you can touch the boards. Yes, please, everyone hug the boards like they are your teddy bear." I end up with a wagon train of kids moving with entropy momentum, all round the edge of the rink, mitts attached to the board like they are stuck to a rope tow. Just like life in general. As long as you can put one foot in front of the other you are making progress.

* * *

My power skating boys at least know their alphabet, the names and locations of most of their body parts, general geometry and what a blue line is. What they don't have is any semblance of order. But I have a whistle and they have already developed a finely-honed Pavlovian response to whistles.

The objective of power skating class is to teach aspiring hockey players to skate efficiently and with purpose. Which is to say, a complete fool's errand. My class is full of tween-age boys, all elbows and knock-knees, incapable of moving in a straight line. Which is probably why they have been entrusted to my skating prowess. But at least they are able to assemble at centre ice without a map, and they are competitive, which in this case equates to being mostly willing to cooperate with orders issued from a skinny girl in a ridiculous flippy-skirted skating outfit, as long as it involves showing off. "I want you all to skate to the end of the rink as fast as you can. Whoever touches the boards first wins!" I say. The group takes off with ice chunks flying, not an elegant side glide among them. They probably all spent their formative years perfecting learn-to-skate's straight-line forward shuffle, which does not bode well for mastering the hockey stop or the crosscut. Luckily, kids all make their own way to the arena: no parents in the stands to critique my teaching style or ask for special accommodation for their child because he is afraid of ice.

The hockey stop is a sharp-edged maneuver with both skates hugging each other, digging in on an acute angle to the torso, with softly bent knees if you don't want to launch yourself head first onto the ice. Hard hockey ice, in the era when wearing helmets is at best optional and at worst wimpy. The trick is mastering it in a manner that flies as close to the flame of perfection as possible without achieving a concussion. My class loves the hockey stop. It's just like what Gordie Howe does when he goes back to the bench after a hat trick. Correctly executed, it results in a tsunami of ice-snow that hits you square in the face as you skate through it. You can't see anything, but at least if you are stationary and vertical you know you've stopped. At which point, you hope like hell the snow-blind person behind you has also figured out how to stop. I run them through the drill over and over again: skate full speed down the length of the rink, end with a hockey stop just shy of the boards. The boys are giddy with aspirations of NHL glory and are silently practising what they'll say when they get pulled over to comment after the playoff game. "I couldn't have done it without the hockey stop I learned in power skating." I'd like to think, anyhow.

My skating may not be Mozart worthy, but I'm damn good at what serves as the scales: inside and outside edges, crosscuts, and of course, hockey stops. My hockey stop could clear the bench. Plus, there's an official card from the Canadian Figure Skating Association in my wallet saying I'm a professional figure skater. That's gotta mean I'm going places. If only from one blue line to the other.

20

The DRW

We launch ourselves through the back door into the Dixon's kitchen, four girls full of after school angst and gossip. Mrs. Dixon is on the evening nursing shift today, so she's sitting at the table busy with her trifecta of smoking, knitting and soaking her bunions in a hot water foot bath. There's tea waiting in a metal pot on the element at the back of the stove, as tannic and viscous as crude oil. Hot water and three more teabags get added every few hours, whether it's needed or not. "The way you girls are dressed you must think it's summer! Go get yourselves some tea," she says in her Irish lilt, "it's cold out there. Fresh brown bread on the sideboard."

I'm very proud of my red, knee high, "wet look" winter boots, with three-inch heels that take the prize for least practical winter boot for a location that actually has winter. They don't offer any warmth or ice traction and their "wet look" status is unfortunately literal, as they aren't waterproof either. But they look really cool with my midi coat, which is called a midi coat because it ends mid-calf. It's black with a zipper trimmed with red and white braid that runs all the way down the front and has a hood that only stays up if there is zero wind. There is never zero wind, a fact that is frequently reinforced by my zipper, which is an ideal wind sanctuary. I'm freezing. I'm not going to admit that myself, let alone Mrs. Dixon.

But Mrs. Dixon is more concerned about my spiritual health than today's frostbite. She regularly foists the most enticing reading material the Catholic Church has to offer in my direction: a tract called *Our Daily Bread* that I'm supposed to read each day to deepen my religiosity and save my immortal soul from purgatory, because I go to the Community Church, which is certainly not Mrs. Dixon's idea of God-sanctioned Christianity. "Gee, thanks, Mrs. Dixon," I say, "I'll read it every day." Meanwhile, I hope to God my mother doesn't find this in my school bag. Forget about purgatory, I'll be inhabiting hell on earth.

"Honestly, where did you get this horrible stuff? You know your great-great-grandparents got driven out of Ireland by those Catholics. I don't think you want to walk down that crooked path. Nothing good would come of it," my mother would be sure to say.

Debbie, Ruth, Julie and I call ourselves the Deep River Women, a.k.a. the DRW. The Deep River part is completely true. The "women" part is aspirational. We call ourselves the DRW because Ruth came across a record in the library called *Deep River Woman*. "Couldn't you just see it if we called ourselves the Deep River Women?" Julie says. I guess we think if we have an official name we are a force to be reckoned with. Except that we're the only ones who know we are official. But maybe that's better. It makes us a secret society.

"Okay," says Ruth. "If we are going to be a secret society, we need proper nicknames. I will be Ruthee. Deb, you will be Deb. Julie, you will be Jule." And I am stuck with Marlinee. Our secret society headquarters is the Dixon's house, because identical twins Debbie and Ruth are half the quorum. Part of the admission to the secret club is being able to tell them apart, despite their identical round glasses, identical long, thick, brown hair, and identical voices. Somehow, I have managed to figure this out. It's kind of like the optical illusion puzzle where you see either a vase or a woman's face. I can now seamlessly navigate Mother Nature's attempt at deception, moving between the woman and the vase without squinting much.

I didn't meet the Dixon twins until grade 9, even though they live only a few streets away from me, just down the block from Julie who I've known since grade school. The Dixons went to Catholic school and besides, even though their dad works at the plant, he's what's called technical, not professional. He's a tool and die maker who manufactures things you can actually see, like the gauges that show when the reactor is reacting badly, so I'm thinking that's kind of important. In the army he'd be an enlisted man not an officer. At least that's what my dad says. Mr. and Mrs. Dixon don't hang out at the curling club or the golf club or the yacht club. I think that's maybe because they have six kids. Debbie and Ruth tell me their mother wanted to call them Deirdre and Fiona, a nomenclature vetoed by Mr. Dixon, who pointed out (likely quite rightly), this would doom them to going through life as Fifi and DeeDee. Instead, Mr. Dixon refers to his oldest kids constantly and collectively by one word: "Debirooth."

Debbie and Ruth have an after-school self-improvement agenda for me that does not involve religion. Or actually that's not quite right. It does involve religion: worshipping at the altar of beauty, an achievement we firmly believe is completely unattainable for us, but we are not unwilling to try our best in case a miracle happens. Trying involves using me as the prototype, focusing attention on my most obvious shortcomings: eyebrows that meet in the middle and the fact I weigh less than seven Christmas's worth of turkey. "How do you expect to ever get boobs if you don't gain weight? Do you even want to get out of the children's section of the Simplicity pattern books? Honestly, you look like you're in grade 6! High school boys have certain standards. You have to suffer to reveal your real beauty." Ruth goes to work whipping up the proprietary Dixon formula for weight gain that's probably the same one used with the Yorkshire terriers Mrs. Dixon breeds, if they don't gain weight fast enough to go out for sale at ten weeks. Ruth hands me a mug of warm milk with something mixed into it that tastes like pureed plankton with a side order of Elmer's glue. "That's Horlicks. It's got barley and malt and seaweed extract and stuff like that. It'll put meat on your bones in no time." Yes, but only if I don't barf it up first, and so far, every indication is that barfing is highly likely. "Deb, go find the tweezers and the magnifying mirror. Those eyebrows are not a sight for sore eyes. If we don't deal with them now, you'll be Frida Kahlo by next week."

Debbie is the eyebrow artiste. She rifles through the pages of the *Seventeen* magazine until she reaches the Mary Quant makeup ad with a big photo of Twiggy, who's flogging the latest must-have shade of blue eyeshadow. "That's what we want. Just a thin line with a little bit of shape. Marlinee, tilt your head back and I'll get to work. This will be a challenge but I think I'm up to it. It shouldn't hurt that much." You're up to it? How about me? The tweezers tweeze away, each eyebrow hair emitting a last gasp of bee sting. They're just dead cells and true to form they're departing as if they're happier to remain lying down.

Ruth and Julie are busy dissecting today's biology class dissection, while waiting for the eyebrow renovation reveal.

"What's with the thing about dissecting worms?" Julie says. "Who doesn't know what a worm looks like inside? And don't the ones at school absolutely reek of formaldehyde? Wouldn't it be funny if we just went and brought one of those Styrofoam containers full of worms you can get out of the fridge up at Jordie's gas station, right next to the milk?" Ruth does think this is funny.

Mrs. Dixon snorts, puts out her cigarette and says, "You girls stop your foolishness and please get the potatoes peeled and in the pot. They're not going to cook themselves. I'm off to work in an hour and Dad and your brother will be wanting supper on the table by five."

Debbie is ready to display her handy work. She has managed to coax my facial Siamese twins into two independent eyebrows, each consisting of a perfect arc, two or three brow hairs thick, stretching from my inner eye to my outer eye, edged with red botches that might serve as a distraction from my zits. "Here," Debbie says, "use this witch hazel. It will be fine by morning. Nobody will notice."

But Debbie has forgotten to factor in my mother when it comes to noticing stuff. "What has happened to your lovely eyebrows?" my mother says, when I slink into the house just before dinner time. "They'll never grow back properly! Honestly, those Dixon girls are a ridiculous influence. Why do you hang around there after school anyway?" I hope she's right. I hope they don't grow back "properly."

* * *

The health club entrance is around a side door at the back corner of Alder House, on the hill behind the high school. Alder House dates from about 1950 and used to be one of the

AECL residences for visiting and single employees, but nobody in their right mind would want to live there now, with its cracked asbestos siding, flaking plaster walls, and bathrooms that are thoroughly modern only if you're stuck in a backwards time warp. These days, the building is relegated to house the library and the health club. The health club is hidden away like there's something shameful about exercising. Maybe it's just that exercising indoors is shameful, when there's perfectly good outdoors outside. Or maybe exercising is more shameful than reading. "Health club" is a serious misnomer for this establishment. It's a tiny room with wonky wood floors and a pervasive ancient sweat smell, almost as bad as the one that envelops the boys' gym at school. There's also an undertone of pee, either mouse or human or both.

The DRW belong to the health club because, in the waning years of high school, if you belong to the health club you are exempt from gym. If you are exempt from gym, you don't have to subject yourself to Mrs. Brown offering helpful critiques to your badminton serve or marking you on how many basketballs you can dunk in thirty seconds. "You girls are completely lame. Pick up your game! Move those butts in those bloomers! I'm not getting any younger here!" Julie actually likes Mrs. Brown, but that's just because Mrs. Brown likes her. Julie is five foot ten, has her swimming Bronze Medallion and works as a life guard in the summer, the type of girl who's actually worthy of gym class. I barely squeezed through Junior Red Cross and my short career as an alternate on the cheerleading squad does not even register in Mrs. Brown's peripheral vision.

Clearly nobody on the high school phys ed staff has ever been to the health club. Or maybe they have and are sniggering in the gym office, thinking it won't be long before we become totally disgusted and report back to gym class, begging for more badminton. To be fair, the health club does the best it can given what it has to work with. Which isn't saying much. It has a stack of thick vinyl floor mats that are never swabbed down, and any foam stuffing that threatens to escape is corralled in with electrical tape by some invisible health club elf, who does nothing else in the maintenance department. The sets of metal dumbbells have had some of their mates run off under cover of darkness to seek a better life, but you do have the option of using the barbells if you are more Charles Atlas inclined. There's also an analogue exercise bicycle that looks like somebody's dad bolted an ancient CCM to blocks of wood salvaged from an abandoned fix-it project. The state-of-the-art of exercise excellence is one of those machines with the vibrating belt that's supposed to shake fat into submission, while you occupy yourself with more important things, like reading a book.

The health club is co-ed, with separate hours for women and men because there's only one communal change room, one communal shower and one communal sauna. The men's and women's hours alternate by week, and just like the timetable at school, are equally as impossible to remember. There is no lock on the health club door. Nobody would bother to try to steal the health club's version of fitness. The protocol, if you are a girl, is to knock loudly before you enter and shout out, "Any men in here?" Most times this doesn't work. Seems like the men don't care if they're naked and high school girls walk in on them.

The DRW go to the health club after school or on weekend evenings. We rarely have dates to infringe on our Saturday night and we don't like watching the hockey game. Neither the one on CBC, nor the one at the arena. I spend enough time at the arena with skating practice as it is. Debbie, Ruth, Julie and I do our diligent workouts of arm curls, lunges, sit ups and stretches. Debbie is adamant about sufficient use of the dumbbells. "No bingo arms for us," she says. "When I see you guys forty years from now your triceps better not be flapping around or I'll disown you! Fifteen more dips!"

"Couldn't you just see it if they had pink dumbbells for girls and blue ones for boys? Only to be subversive, we'd use the blue ones except maybe nobody would know we'd used the blue ones instead of the pink ones because there's never anyone here to notice and then what would be the point?" says Julie.

After the mandatory exercises, we each demonstrate our special skill, the one we trot out if anyone else dares to enter the health club when we're in attendance, to scare them away with our physical prowess. Ruth can fold herself into a perfect seated front bend, collapsing into a horizontal body shape that's almost completely flat. Debbie can do a back walkover, bending backwards into a "C" shape on the mat, then kicking her right leg straight up to the ceiling to propel herself backwards, landing steadily on her feet. Julie can clasp her hands behind her back, bend over and raise her palms all the way towards the ceiling. When I sit with the soles of my feet together, heels wedged into my crotch, my knees touch the ground without any human intervention. We practice the one thing we're good at over and over, to remind ourselves we are actually good at something, even if it's something that will only ever be useful at the gym. But our superpowers combined form one superhero who's not to be messed with. The DRW.

After a workout that Mrs. Brown would likely find sorely lacking, we hit the shower *en masse*. We don't mind being naked together. Who else will ever see us naked anyway?

Debbie maintains her diligence at monitoring our physical appearance so that it hovers as close as it can to her version of the minimally acceptable standard. "Pits and pegs, girls. Shaving. Every. Single. Day. Julie, what's up with those pubes? I know you're blonde but really, this summer you have to deal with the bathing suit overflow. And Marlinee, is that a mustache I see sprouting? Listen, I just found a new thing at the drugstore. It's called Jolen Crème Bleach. Let's do that after school next week. It will be fun! And it works for arms too!" Can't wait, I think.

We head on to the sauna, a wooden room that's always as dankly warm as a rainforest, except the rainforest probably doesn't have mildew in the corners. Despite its dubious cleanliness, the sauna is the highlight of the health club in the winter. "Couldn't you just see it if we lived in the sauna all winter? I wouldn't mind prune fingers if I could just be this warm until spring," says Julie.

We clomp home through the winter dark on a February Saturday night. The hockey game is already well decided, if not completely done. My wet hair is frozen into Popsicles, my face steaming, my core temperature still warm enough from the sauna that my coat is unzipped. Boyfriends, schmoyfriends.

21

Driving Me Crazy

My bicycle pretty much takes me where I want to go, as long as where I want to go is within bicycle distance. Which is to say, anywhere in town. Getting out of town requires a bus or a car. There is no train or plane. Everyone's parents have a car. One car. Gaining access to the car is like solving a quadrilateral equation made up entirely of unknowns, because it depends on the number of siblings of driving age, divided by the number of parental golf games, multiplied by the probability of curling bonspiels. But despite the scarcity of car access, everybody learns to drive as soon as the law says they can.

To learn to drive legally, you need to acquire a "365" learners permit that's good for a year. Sometime during the year, you are expected to take (and pass) a driver's test. I don't know what happens if you let the three hundred and sixty-five days expire without a test, because I don't think that has ever happened. The 365 is earned based on a written test. The written test is based on *The Driver's Handbook*, a three-by-five-inch paperback booklet published by the province, with one hundred and seventy-seven pages. The test is held twice a year, spring and fall.

Everybody within spitting distance of their sixteenth birthday shows up. Including me. Swept along with the crowd of my car-bit-champing peers.

I don't bother to read *The Driver's Handbook*, as its one hundred and seventy-seven pages of stuff to do with driving do not hold much reading appeal. Plus, for some reason, there is a limited number of *Driver's Handbooks* to go around, and they get passed from kid to kid to kid until they disintegrate, so finding one intact is pretty much impossible.

I register for the fall test, which is held after school in the typing room. Not a single page of *The Driver's Handbook* has sullied my eyes. I'm quite proud of this achievement since a lot of single pages are floating around. There's a sign in sheet at the door, where a woman hands me a question book and answer sheet. I go into the room and slide into a desk beside Susan. Carol, Glen, Billy and Rhonda are also already in the room. "Psst," I say. "Did you guys read the handbook?" They all move their heads up and down.

Mr. Wilson's at the front of the room getting ready to proctor the test. "Okay," he says. "No talking. When you're done, bring your answer sheet to me and sit quietly at your desk until everyone else is finished."

I open my test and get started. It's multiple choice. Easy-peasy. I pass if I get forty out of fifty correct. They won't even be subtracting the wrongs from the rights like Mr. Wilson normally does! I just need to make sure I don't choose too many of the same letter in a row. That's never the right way to do it. The first few questions are simple. What colour is a stop sign? When do you use your windshield wipers? How do you indicate a turn? Really, who would need to read a book to know this stuff?

I continue to multiple-guess my way through the test and finally hit the last question. "Where do you drive on the road: The left. The right. The middle. The shoulder." Well duh! Shouldn't you drive in the middle of your lane? The third answer has got to be what they're after. I walk up to the front of the room and hand my answer sheet to Mr. Wilson with a flourish.

"I'll mark these tonight and post the results outside the principal's office tomorrow morning." Mr. Wilson says. Okay. I've nailed it, I think.

The next day, I head down the hall from my locker and see a bunch of kids huddled around the principal's bulletin board. It's the list of names that passed the 365 test. Carol's on it, Glen's on it. Susan's on it. Billy's on it. Rhonda's on it. "Where's your name?" says Susan. Wait, where is my name? There must be a mistake. I run up the stairs to the typing room, two steps at a time. In three-inch platform shoes. Mr. Wilson is taking the covers off the typewriters.

"Mr. Wilson, I'm not on the 365 list," I say.

"That's because only those who passed the test are on the list." he says. "And you definitely did not pass. You can try again in the spring."

Good thing only Carol, Glen, Susan, Rhonda and Billy know I didn't pass. I go back down to collect my books for first period. Angela's waiting outside my locker. "Too bad you flunked the 365," she says. Oh, right. Angela knew I was taking the test.

I pass Ruth in the hall. "How did you manage to muck up the 365?" she says. Oh right. Ruth knew I was taking the test.

I head to English class and sit down behind Julie. She turns around and says, "I said to Ruth, couldn't you just see it if Marlinee doesn't pass the 365?"

After school, I get on my bike and head home. "Hey loser," my brother says. "Everyone at school says you bombed out on the 365. It's easy-peasy. What are you, retarded?"

"Shut up, moron," I say. I like my bike. No big deal.

And maybe I'm on to something. Mr. White comes into Geography class looking glum. "The Arab petroleum exporters are very annoyed at countries like ours that supported Israel during the Yom Kippur War. OAPEC is turning the oil tap down to a trickle," he says. "We have to start using more of our own oil. By my calculation, we'll be out of domestic petroleum by 1980. This is the end of the era of cheap gas. If I had to guess, I'd bet nobody will own a car by then. We'll all just be sharing one neighbourhood car for emergencies only. It's the worst disaster of our time."

The price of gas doubles the next day to fifty-three cents. Nobody can borrow their dad's car unless they pay for gas. Suddenly, a lot of bikes come out of retirement.

* * *

Angela got her licence last year and she can even drive a standard transmission, but she only gets to drive her dad's Dodge station wagon when she goes to her part-time job at the gas station up the highway, where she can fill up on employee gas. But that's okay, her boyfriend Keith has his own car. He has a car because he lives in Chalk River and is in grade 12, past the point at which it's way too lame to take the school bus. Keith's car is a 1960 Sunbeam that cost him two hundred bucks, the only car that he could get with the proceeds of his summer job. Angela's parents don't seem to mind that he's from out of town and isn't even going to do grade 13. Angela gets away with a lot more than I do, probably because she irons creases in her jeans and wears Love's Baby Soft instead of Coty Wild Musk. Her parents don't even know she listens to Alice Cooper and Black Sabbath with Keith downstairs in the rec room with the lights out. They think she's a goody-good.

Angela and I used to be joined at the hip until she started always having a boyfriend. But I've put my bike away for the season so Keith agrees to drop me off when he takes Angela home from school. Angela sometimes feels sorry for my lack of girlfriend status and invites me to tag along with them. Or maybe she's trying to show me how the whole girlfriend–boyfriend thing is done, a lesson that's a bit hard to absorb from my perch in the middle of the back seat. I'm on the bench in more ways than one, but at least I can say I've been a cheerleader.

Angela fiddles with the car radio to try and pull in a station. "There's a new Rolling Stones out," she says. "This is stupid!" All we can normally get during daylight hours is the country station from Pembroke, which plays Charley Pride and Loretta Lynn, interspersed with local talent like The Family Brown, who also have a TV show on the Pembroke CBC repeater station that's on right before the hockey game. "The Family Brown! Honestly! That ten-year-old Tracey girl has been ten years old for the past four years!" says Angela. She's right, I think. Or maybe it's just reruns. Who would know? It's the same show every time. Papa Joe Brown tells some stupid joke. He introduces ten-year-old Tracey, they launch into their one hit, "Raised on Country Music," then Papa Joe tells some other stupid joke, then they play a Kenny Rogers song. And on and on until the theme from Hockey Night in Canada kicks in. I kind of like country music, though I would never say that out loud. If raised on country music means that's the only thing other than CBC you can pull in on the AM radio for your entire formative years, I guess I qualify.

Johnny Cash has finished walking the line when the radio says: "Let's all go to A&W, food's more fun, at A&W. I can taste it now, can't you? Hop in the car! Come as you are! To A&W."

"Hey. Let's do it. The radio says we should! You guys got gas money?" says Keith. We have never been to a fast food restaurant. The A&W is in Pembroke. Where fake ten-year-old Tracey lives. Forty miles away. Population 9,000, twice as big as our town. I scrounge around in the back pocket of my jeans and retrieve a crumpled dollar bill. That'll get us about three-quarters of the way there. We head up to the highway and turn east towards A&W like it's a homing beacon. Bobby Goldsboro cuts in and out on the radio, singing about trees and how big they've grown. Really? Bobby Goldsboro knows about trees? We could teach him a thing or two.

We pass the rolling sand dunes of the Champlain Sea. The flagpoles beside the road on the Petawawa plains near the army base fly square, solid red flags, indicating live ammunition in use. Artillery booms in the distance and tanks line the dirt road that runs parallel to the old railway line beside the highway. Angela continues to mess with the radio dial. "Hey," she says, "I think we've got something!"

We start singing along with Mick Jagger. Something about wild horses. Oh yes, they could drag me away, I think.

When we finally get to Pembroke, it's almost five. My mother is going to give me heck when I get home. "Just say you were at my house and forgot what time it was," says Angela. We pull up, park in the A&W drive-in lanes and wait for the carhop to take our order. Root beer. Whistle Dogs. My dinner is totally going to be spoiled. I hope we're having liver and onions tonight. Keith cranks the car window halfway down and the carhop hooks the tray over the top of the glass. He reaches into the back seat to heft me my root beer in a tall, thick glass mug that's as frosty as the inside of my bedroom window in January. I have no idea what root beer is, but if this is what it is, I'm a believer. Angela distributes the Whistle Dogs, fancy hotdogs wrapped in bacon with melted cheese on a squishy white bun. Mustard if you want it. A store-boughten party in my mouth. The A&W sign flashes orange neon. Sitting in cars around us, people are laughing, talking, eating burgers. A&W pumps a happy soundtrack out into the parking lot: "The Twist," "Twist and Shout," "Peppermint Twist." Food is definitely more fun here. Everything is more fun here. The radio was right.

Keith's dashboard clock only tells the correct time twice a day: midnight and noon. I have no idea what time it is, but likely closer to midnight than noon. Angela does not seem concerned. "I'm at Keith's for dinner, then working at the hardware store tonight," she says. "Not expected home." Easy for her to say. We finish our fast-food feast and spend the next hour retracing our way back to town. I leave the Cinderella finery of Pembroke behind and prepare to re-enter my life of drudgery. It's starting to get dark. In the twilight, the Champlain Sea's vestigial moguls on the side of the road look like camels losing their battle with the Sahara, undulating west, trying their best to get somewhere that's not here, only they don't know the best they can do is end up in Mattawa.

22

Fine Dining

It always seems that each new decade doesn't really start coming into its own until several years into it. By 1973, the '70s were finally ready to flex their muscles. The Beatles had broken up. The Vietnam War was limping towards its messy conclusion. Disco was elbowing its way on to the charts. And eaters were finally ready to lose their vice-like grip on meat-and-two-veg. Gourmet cooking had arrived. Gourmet was anything that involved sauce or exotic ingredients, like garlic and wine.

My mother is fully on the fancy food bandwagon and is taking gourmet cooking at night school. "We can eat at home like we're dining out at the Chateau Laurier in Ottawa," she says."

On Tuesdays and Thursdays when she goes to the high school home ec room, dad makes us wieners and beans or frozen meat pies. The meat pies are always burned on the top, soggy on the bottom, and still partly frozen in the middle. "Just eat the cooked bits," my dad says. "Many a poor man could make a good meal out of this." I hope my mother aces her course.

Each week, my mother brings home new recipes. Coq au vin. Quiche. Borscht. Beef Wellington. Vichyssoise. Every weekend she serves us one of her new recipes, each of which is full of the promise of a new decade of sophisticated palates. Then we never see them again. "Too much work," she says. Then it's back to baked ham and scalloped potatoes and meatloaf and spaghetti sauce and Sunday roast beef. And peas. Lots of peas. I hate each and every dinner.

* * *

Every table at the Deep River Restaurant and Tavern is decked out with paper placemats that have scalloped edges and advertising around the perimeter. "Deep River Motel: Open Year-Round." I'm glad they point that out, because clearly not closing in the winter is a renegade move. "Laurentian View Dairy: Quality is our motto. Milk, cream, butter, eggs, skim milk, buttermilk, chocolate milk, cottage cheese, orange juice." I get the dairy parts of this list, but the eggs and orange juice are little at odds with the dairy thing. But maybe it's a breakfast marketing angle. "Figaro's Men's Hairstylists: Specialists in Razor Cuts. Styles to suit individual taste. The Proud Man Salon." And what could possibly be wrong with that, except maybe the use of capitalization.

In the mid-field of the Deep River Restaurant placemats, there are pictures of cocktails nobody ever orders. The cocktails are as fancy as Easter eggs, pink, green, sweet and frothy, with cherries on top or half-rounds of orange on the side of a glass that borrowed its curves from Mae West. Even if anyone ever ordered one, I sincerely doubt any cocktail would measure up to its publicity photo. The Deep River Restaurant (and Tavern) is on the highway, just east of the "Welcome to Deep River" sign. Because of that, it's probably not officially in town, but no one would mistake it for being anywhere else, since anywhere else is a long way away. If you fail to pull into the DRR (&T) on your westward journey on Highway 17, your edible food options run out until you hit Mattawa, unless it's summer, in which case you can fill up on chips from the chip truck that can usually be found in the parking lot of Crowder's Shell gas station (and auto centre). Another placemat advertiser.

Restauranteurs in the far-flung corners of the country are invariably Chinese or Greek. Our restaurant proprietors are Spiros and George from somewhere in Greece. It's a mystery how they ended up running a pizza joint and "family" restaurant on the Trans-Canada Highway north of Algonquin Park, but their presence is likely due to the witness protection program or a severe allergy to the Mediterranean sun. Spiros is the front of the house, while George cranks out the cheeseburgers, banquet burgers, and hot roast beef sandwiches behind a pass-through with a bell on the counter and a length of clothesline pinned with yellow order slips.

Before Spiros and George saved us from our culinary wasteland, my exposure to pizza was limited to do-it-yourself boxes of Chef Boyardee, so anything was bound to be an improvement. Greece is kind of near Italy, at least the bottom bits are, but George has his own spin on what a pizza should be. The DRR pizza has pepperoni, mushrooms and green peppers, but after that it veers off into territory never before trodden by a pizza. The toppings are diced very finely, admittedly a testament to George's knife skills, then mixed in with the cheese. There's a thin smear of tomato sauce on the dough, providing just a hint of red before the homogenous mix of topping and cheese goes on. The cooked result is an undifferentiated mass of very brown cheesy stuff on top of a crust that is pleasantly greasy. Chef Boyardee, you are dead to me.

Ruth has a job at the DRR as a waitress this summer. She is issued a short-sleeved gold polyester dress with patch pockets on the front, one to hold her order pad and the other to hold her change float. It hangs straight down from the shoulders and ends mid-calf, the better to accommodate the Platonic form of a Greek grandmother. "I am so not wearing this," she says, and hacks the dress off just below the pockets to create a tunic. "I'm going to zip down to Ritters and get some of the same material to make some pants," she says. The resulting outfit is so far from stylish it could be on the cover of the Sears catalogue. "Who cares?" she says. "At least none of the customers will hit on me." In addition to her day shift that ends at four, Spiros calls Ruth to come in when it gets busy on weekend nights. The DRW are sitting in the Dixon's kitchen deciding what to do with our Friday night when the phone rings. "Hello, Root? You come in work, few hours?"

"Sure, Spiros," Ruth says. "I'll be there by six-thirty." She hangs up and says, "Darn it. How come he didn't know it was busy when I left? I just changed out of my charming work clothes. Why don't you guys come up for pizza later? You're not doing anything else anyhow." Thanks for the vote of confidence in our ability to generate evening plans, Ruth.

Debbie, Julie and I ride our bikes eastbound on the shoulder of the highway in the dusty gravel. My thin tires don't offer much cushioning, but at least I can out run most of the mosquitos. The car headlights briefly light our way as they head westward. Every time we pass a house, a mixed-breed dog runs to the end of his choke-chain tether, barking like we're trying to steal the family TV. When we get to the restaurant, we lean our bikes up against the side of the building, and go in to claim a booth. Ruth waves in our direction and hurries away to deliver orders to tables.

George clangs the bell every two minutes. "Root! Pick food. Root! Pick pizza. Root!"

"I'm off shift in two minutes, George," Ruth says. "Spiros, tell George I'm off!" She grabs a pizza from the pass-through and brings it over to our table. "Nobody picked up this takeout order," she says. "Spiros told them 'fifteen minute, be ready' and it's already been half an hour." Ruth sits down and tells us about her night. "My feet feel like my mother's. And you will not believe this," she says. "Spiros asked me to go to the movies with him! I said I can't, I have a boyfriend. Spiros! He has to be thirty years old! And besides, you know that the ketchup in the Heinz bottles is really just filled up from a vat in the kitchen. He's too cheap to buy the real thing. Do they even have ketchup in Greece?"

"Couldn't you just see it if you married Spiros and moved to Greece?" says Julie. Ruth does not think this is funny.

We sit on Friday night with someone else's pizza. Someone else who was probably having so much fun they forgot to pick it up. And the only person asking anyone out is Spiros.

Debbie's waitress job is at Jordie's diner, attached to the BP gas station. It has two advantages over Ruth's job: it's on the highway but it's right at the top of Deep River Road and it closes at seven. It's a narrow room that has cracked green vinyl stools attached to the floor in front of the counter, and chrome-legged tables and chairs by the window, for those who prefer not to have a front row seat to witness how the burgers are made. Debbie's job is to fetch the western omelets, burgers, and fries from the counter and plop them down on the tables. She has a coffee carafe surgically attached to her left hand and a pencil permanently perched above her right ear.

Danny mans the flattop. An apron that used to be white is tied around his waist and hangs down to his knees. He has a blue ink tattoo of an anchor on his left forearm and always has a cigarette in his mouth. I don't know how he lights it, because his hands are always busy flipping eggs, burgers and grilled cheese sandwiches. He scrapes the grease into a trough at the front of the grill, which is slanted to drain down somewhere. Nobody ever asks where. Least of all Debbie.

The rumour is that Danny was in jail and that's how he learned to cook. This is kind of believable, since I can imagine the type of food he knows how to "cook" would be very popular in jail. Danny is not the kind of person you would ask to confirm or deny this rumour, though. Debbie says Danny never says much of anything. Maybe because his mouth is usually full of cigarette. "Say what you will about Danny," Debbie says. "He pays me cash every Thursday and at least he hasn't asked me out." Hmmm, I think. Is that a good thing or bad thing? Does that mean the DRW aren't even good enough for Danny the jailbird?

* * *

The dairy isn't exactly a restaurant but it's certainly a destination. It's on the highway on the west side of town. Mr. Blimke used to deliver our milk every week in glass bottles with a cardboard tab for a lid and when the cream on top froze in the winter, it would pop like a cork and push the cardboard up over the top of the bottle. He used to come every week, but if for some bizarre reason you didn't want milk, you put a sign in your window that said "No Milk." Herman's Hermits even had a song called "No Milk Today," and maybe that's where Mr. Blimke got the idea, but I don't think so. Mr. Blimke seems like more of a Family Brown guy. He also delivered other stuff purveyed by the dairy including Beep, a weird combination of orange, prune, apricot, apple and pineapple juices in a one-quart carton with sugar and orange dye #12 as listed as its first two ingredients. But now you can buy all the Laurentian View Dairy stuff from the A&P, so Mr. Blimke just stays put at the dairy and does other dairy things. Whatever they are.

The main reason to go to the dairy is the ice cream. They even have a fancy dessert called the Atomic Special, which is four scoops of ice cream (one for each reactor), covered in chocolate, raspberry, blueberry sauce, probably to imitate the outcome of a meltdown that does not involve ice cream. Mrs. Blimke runs the ice cream counter, which is filled to capacity with twelve tubs of the dairy's finest flavours du jour. She wields the metal scoop with her well-nourished upper arms flapping jauntily in the summer breeze. There's always tiger tail, and it's probably the one and only tub of tiger tail the dairy has every produced, because nobody ever orders it. Or maybe the same people order it as those who order fancy drinks at the DRR, so slyly and stealthily that it escapes notice. Tiger tail is neon orange ice cream with a black licorice stripe. It is truly disgusting. The only right thing to order is maple walnut, made with maple syrup that's from just down the road. Ruth does not agree. She always gets chocolate. Debbie always gets strawberry. Julie always gets mint because mint is healthy. Even though our order is always the same, it takes at least ten minutes of rumination in front of Mrs. Blimke's ice cream counter to make our decision, while Mrs. Blimke cleans her ice cream scoop impatiently.

"Oh look. They have peach today," says Debbie. "And blueberry. And strawberry."

"Couldn't you just see it if I had one scoop of vanilla and one of mint?" says Julie. We never get two scoops. Today or any other day. Julie orders her mint. Single scoop.

You can have your scoop in the regular cone, a light beige flat-bottomed cylinder with a larger circular bit on top that holds the ice cream, which melts down through the bottom if you don't eat it fast enough. Or you can pay extra for a sugar cone. The sugar cone is like the photogenic ice cream cones you see in movies: a proper cone-shaped cone that's golden brown and all waffle-y on the outside. Ready for its close-up. We never cough up for the sugar cone. Nobody ever does. Or maybe only the people who order the tiger tail ice cream. The sugar cones have dust on them and always will.

Mrs. Blimke hands us our cones and we eat them on the way home, walking our water buffalo sandals down the highway shoulder, licking ice cream that's threatening to run down our forearms. We dash across the highway when we get to Deep River Road, dodging the Trans-Canada traffic where the speed limit temporarily drops from sixty to fifty miles per hour. There is no stoplight here nor anywhere else in town. We stay true to Mr. Bland's vision. A suburb without a city.

23

Highways and Byways

The Elms Hotel is on the highway right across from Deep River Road, the eastern entrance to town. The Elms is one of those hotels that has rooms but nobody ever seems to stay in them. And maybe the Elms would like to keep it that way. Its real purpose in life is the beverage room. Or to be more accurate, the beverage rooms: one for men and one for "ladies and escorts." The men's side is dingy and smoky, tables slick with beer pitcher sweat, cluttered with dead-soldier draft glasses.

The side deemed appropriate for "ladies" is dingy and smoky, tables slick with beer pitcher sweat, cluttered with dead-soldier draft glasses. But it has a shuffleboard table in case the ladies and their escorts want to get covered in sawdust. Escorts are optional, though. By the 1970s, the liquor law has evolved enough to permit a group of ladies to enjoy their beverages without benefit of a Y chromosome. But the liquor law has not yet evolved to admit sixteen-year-olds like me. As far as my parents are concerned, I'm over at the Dixon's watching TV and plucking my eyebrows.

I will operate under the assumption that we have passed the statute of limitations for everything and everyone involved. In my own defence and in defence of all of my fellow underage patrons that hung out in the taverns on the highway, where else were we supposed to go?

There are two things to eat at the Elms Hotel and none of them is breakfast, lunch or dinner. There are pickled eggs in a jar on the top of the bar counter that have more of a decorative than culinary appeal (using the words "decorative," "culinary" and "appeal" very loosely), and chuckwagons. Chuckwagons are ham and processed cheese sandwiches on a hotdog bun wrapped in cellophane. When hunger desperation strikes, you procure a chuckwagon, put it in a microwave oven provided solely for chuckwagons, press the "chuckwagon" button and nuke it into submission, cellophane and all. The sandwich, if it deserves to be called that, oozes molten orange goo on top of ham that tastes like melted plastic. The bun is satisfyingly squishy, though, and pretty much the highlight of the price of admission, which is about seventy-five cents.

The Elms is the place to be because of the live music and the thirty-cent draft beer and the fact that nobody asks for ID. Ever. It's our version of a teen clubhouse, without the milkshakes or wholesome activities. Of course, I never would have gone to a teen clubhouse with those flavours of attractions, if one had existed. I have my standards.

Debbie, Ruth, Julie and I sit at one of the wood tables marred with rings left by previous generations of beer bottles and drifts of salt from shakers lying on their side in something sticky. The salt is there because patrons put it in their draft, which either has something to do with using chemistry to create a bigger head on the beer or makes it taste less like a skunk smells, or both. But we don't drink beer. We drink ginger ale instead of real ale. We aren't here for the adult beverages, we're here for the band. Still, I'm in a bar when I'm supposed to be watching TV at the Dixon's house. I keep looking around to see if there is someone here who might know me, but I guess hanging out at the Elms is not really my parent's speed. And hopefully not any of their friends' speed either.

Tonight's band, The Checkers, is made up of local boys who crank out covers of whatever was on the chart ten years ago: "The Twist," "Twist and Shout," "Peppermint Twist." Peter, the lead singer, has a ponytail and Lee bootcut jeans that are just about impossible to buy anywhere near this place. We're pretty sure he has no idea any of us exist.

Our out-on-the-town uniform is Howick jeans and t-shirts. We can get Howicks because they are from Ottawa and therefore reasonably local. Our preferred style of Howicks is as wide a leg as possible. A leg that could harbor an elephant with room to spare. The bottom of the legs completely engulf my shoes and I look like a hovercraft when I walk. My t-shirt is homemade tie-dye, manufactured in a bathtub full of Rit cold water dye, at the expense of the colour of the tub and the wrath of my mother, who does not see why I need to wreck a perfectly good white shirt in the process of wrecking the bathtub. "What the heck? Why is the bathtub purple? Honestly, I don't understand you kids!" she says. "What's wrong with that perfectly good pink blouse I got you at Ritter's?" That pink blouse has so many things wrong with it I'd be explaining into next week.

We are stealth groupies masquerading as nerdy girls. But Debbie is extra bold tonight. "I didn't come here to be a wimp. I mean really, I don't have to go out with the first person who asks me, but when is that ever going to happen anyway? I should ask someone out my own damn self. I'm just going to go up there and ask Peter for a request. You guys can just sit here and grow old," she says. This is so embarrassing. What if Peter ignores her? What would she do then? And even worse, what if he decides to be her boyfriend? We do not call attention to ourselves in order to preserve the cone of silence hiding our hideousness. The DRW stick together and Debbie is breaking rank. I sink down in my chair and contemplate slinking off to the bathroom. Either that or I could create a tent with my jeans and hide in them.

The band breaks after the first set. Peter slings his guitar back over his shoulder and heads offstage. "Going for a smoke?" he asks the rest of the band, and they all nod in agreement. I don't think they're talking about cigarettes. Debbie spies her window of opportunity and takes her Howicks over to intercept him before he reaches the side door. She says something and he smiles. He says something and she laughs. They stand chatting for a good five minutes. What the heck?

Debbie finally comes back to the table. We sit in stunned silence. "I asked him if it was okay if I asked him to play 'Have I the Right,'" she says, "And he said, yes you do have the right. He is so hilarious! Then I told him his brother George was in a play with me and he said he saw it and I played a very good Eskimo. And then he said he'd look for me after church on Sunday. I guess that means I can't skip out on church. Darnit. I was supposed to have a piano lesson from Jimmy Dumanoir at the Byeways." Crap! No way she can have a boyfriend!

* * *

Our other local, the Byeways, is literally a roadhouse: a log lodge at the bend in the road that echoes the bend in the Ottawa River at Point Alexander just west of town. In addition to the main lodge, it has a smattering of miniature log cabins available for rent by the hour, day, week or month. The inside of the Byeways is an homage to the log-drivers who plied their trade up and down the river in the early decades of the twentieth century. It has lacquered log walls, pine tables with log legs, pine chairs with log arms and legs, pine floors, a pine ceiling, and pretty much pine on any surface that sits still long enough. The bathrooms have saloon doors and pine toilet seats. Fortunately, they have the good sense not to provide birch bark for toilet paper.

If you go through the front door of the Byeways, you arrive in a semi-respectable dining room where you can get fried pickerel in the summer and fried pickerel in the winter. There's a mural on the wall of the early days of the voyageurs on the Ottawa River, with canoes filled with beaver pelts and savage Indians lining the shore, bows and arrows at the ready. It also has paper placemats and real cutlery and everything, so you know it's a classy dining joint. But why would you ever go through the front door? Most people are not looking for pickerel, so they go in the back door from the parking lot, where you end up in a somewhat less than semi-respectable bar that seems like it's lit by a single forty-watt bulb. The Byeways has the exact same ID policy as the Elms. Don't ask, don't tell. Everyone looks over eighteen in indoor twilight, anyhow.

Nancy, the waitress, wears a short canvas apron that's seen better days, with a pocket where she keeps all her change. She folds her spare bills lengthwise in thirds and winds them around her fingers with the ends pointing away from her palm. Dollar bills on the right hand and two-dollar bills on the left. Nancy isn't a lifelong bar slinger for nothing. She can heft a tray of thirty draft like it's a box of

Kleenex. She is also a master of getting patrons to round up to an even dollar by extending the rummage in her apron for the required coins way past the attention span of the average beer drinker. She probably has the same change float she's had since she started her Byeways career twenty years ago. Same apron, too.

The entertainment attractions at the Byeways, other than the beer, are best described as miss or miss. Jimmy Dumanoir, who lives in one of the housekeeping cabins, plays the piano when he feels like it. But when he does feel like it, his stubby fingers crank out boogie-woogie that would put Jerry Lee Lewis to shame, as he deftly manages to balance a cigarette, with ash intact all the way down to the filter, on the side edge of the piano. Other than that, it's pretty much the jukebox: three plays for twenty-five cents. You can select your songs anytime, but the jukebox will play every quarter ahead of yours first, and of course you don't know what everyone else has already picked. So the jukebox plays "Rocket Man" a thousand times in a row with brief intermissions of "American Pie" and "Brandy."

Sometimes though, we have the strippers. The northern stripper tour comes through town every couple of months as it makes its way through the hotspots: Espanola, Elliot Lake, Timmins and of course, Point Alexander. I don't know where they go after that. They probably continue on to triumphant shows in Cobden and Barry's Bay and maybe all the way to Bancroft.

Somehow, Debbie and I end up at the Byeways on a stripper night. On this particular evening, the stripper du jour is Cathi with an "i," which she probably dots with a heart. I know her name because I met her in the girls' bathroom, which also doubles as the stripper change room. But there's nothing wrong with that. No worse than grade 8 with no gym change room, although her outfit is a little different than what I wore in grade 8. Cathi walks out to her headline gig wearing her stripper costume under a fuzzy pink robe that looks like the kind my mother has. She heads towards the slightly raised platform that serves as a stage, sits down on a stool and finishes her classy Virginia Slim cigarette while she waits until the jukebox runs out of quarters so she can load it up with her own three songs: "Smoke on the Water," "Knock Three Times," and "Gypsys, Tramps and Thieves." We are all very thankful she does not choose "Rocket Man."

Cathi's specialty is a form of fan dance, executed with towels instead. The towels come from the housekeeping cabins: thin, nearly white, as soft as sandpaper and whiffing wafts of Clorox that mingle with the stale, spilled beer. But this is not Cathi's first rodeo. She wields her terry-cloth costume with precision, first doing her best dance interpretation of Deep Purple's description of fire in the sky while swapping the bath towels in front of her torso, followed by miming Tony Orlando knocking on the ceiling and the pipes as she waves the hand towels over her head, then finally dancing to Cher, who is singing about gypsies dancing for the money thrown by an appreciative audience. By this time, Cathi is in the full glory of her jury-rigged facecloth G-string. Nothing I haven't seen at the health club, and even slightly more elegant.

The guys all take the money-throwing thing seriously. They launch handfuls of nickels, dimes and quarters in the direction of the narrow stage, which bounce off the floor, walls and ceiling. Cathi does her best to dodge the silver until Cher shuts up. She bows to the tepid applause, puts on her robe, retrieves her discarded linen from the top of the jukebox, then bends down to gather up the coins. Probably about three bucks max. This does not seem like a good value-proposition to me. Despite the opportunity it presents to travel up and down Highway 17, and the entrepreneurial appeal, I decide I will cross stripper off my list of potential occupations and stick with famous actress, Olympic figure skater or bestselling author. "Rocket Man" begins its umpteenth whirl on the Wurlitzer as Nancy hustles for last call. Her change stash remains intact.

The problem with the Byeways is not just its dodgy reputation. The problem is you need a car to get there. Ruth can drive a standard and sometimes gets to borrow her dad's Dodge station wagon, but generally we need someone to ferry us back and forth. Tonight, as the bar lights get turned to max to signal the end of the night, Arthur and Fred are AWOL, so Debbie and I are left looking for a ride home. Luckily, we see Peter's dad sitting at his usual table in the corner, downing his last call beer with a Duff Gordon brandy chaser. Debbie says, "Hey! That's Mr. King over there! I know him from church. He's mostly drunk so I don't think we'll have a problem bumming a ride." We scuttle across the room, arrive at Mr. King's table, and ask him if he's headed back to town.

He looks up with semi-focused eyes, his plaid shirt buttoned one hole off, his change for Nancy on the table. He says, "Sure girls. I want to make sure you get home safe. Just let me go for a leak then I'll meet you in the parking lot."

Debbie and I go out back and get into his four-door Buick. Mr. King lights up a wine-tipped cigarillo then turtles his way out onto the highway. We turn left towards town and only about two miles later he remembers to turn on the headlights. The speed limit is sixty. We are barely cracking twenty-five on the Trans-Canada Highway. Mr. King drives in slow motion down the road for about twenty minutes, developing an impressive convoy of transport trucks in his wake, until we reach the turn off for Ridge Road, the western entrance to town. His internal autopilot ends at his house, completely the other end from where we need to be. He invites us in for a nightcap, but I am already on the wrong side of explainable absence, so Debbie and I hightail it back up to the highway and hustle it home. No time to snake-and-ladder my way through town from crescent to cul-de-sac. The crow is how I need to fly tonight. If I ever want to get my tie-dyed self out of the house ever again.

24

Fresh Blood

Nuclear power plants are a mystery to most people, perhaps existing only as vaguely vase-shaped concrete vessels, tethered by the stickmen that carry the electrical grid out to the insatiable mouths of furnaces, light bulbs, refrigerators, ovens, televisions, coffee makers and video games. Or perhaps, evoking a vague (or maybe not so vague) sense of unease and foreboding that something could go terribly wrong when neutrons are allowed to careen about with wild abandon.

The choice of how to reign in neutron enthusiasm is the crux of the decision of how to design a nuclear reactor, because apparently there's more than one way to do it. You can use graphite, a particularly stable form of carbon, stability being a virtue when you are about to play goalie to a cloud of rowdy neutrons; you can use beryllium, if you can find it, because it comes into existence only via atomic nuclei that have collided with cosmic rays, and you can wait a long time for that to happen enough times before you finally get enough beryllium to coat the head of a pin; or, you can use plain old water. But plain old water only works if you don't use plain old uranium. Otherwise, you need to "enrich" the uranium with not-so-benign stuff like plutonium (which aside from its radioactivity, is also a heavy metal poison that's as deadly as nerve gas) or thorium (the powdered version of which spontaneously combusts when exposed to air).

Neither AECL nor Ontario Hydro nor Canadian General Electric, the partners in the enterprise of developing a Canadian nuclear power reactor, arrived in this world by falling off a cabbage truck. The U.S. had already chosen graphite as their method of neutron taming, so in the service of advancing atomic science, Canada decided to select another path. Beryllium was deemed too elusive, so water won out. Well, sort of water. Canada wanted to use unenriched uranium for fuel, both because it doesn't come with the expense of enrichment and doesn't leave the door open for co-opting enrichment facilities to produce atomic weapon materials. Supposedly.

So instead of plain old water, they needed "heavy" water. Heavy water is, in absolute terms, no more in need of Weight Watchers than regular water. It just has a lot of deuterium, a form of hydrogen that comes with an extra neutron so it isn't as glutinous in the neutron Pacman business, and it doesn't slow the neutrons down so much that it interferes with the fission thing. In the Goldilocks world of uranium-238, it's just right. And thus, the Canada Deuterium Uranium (CANDU) power reactor was born. The CANDU prototype, called the Nuclear Power Demonstration station (NPD), went live ten miles up the Ottawa River near Rolphton in 1962, bringing the total number of experimental and prototype reactors in the vicinity of Deep River to four.

* * *

Saturday night at the Elms. The Ravens are playing last year's top ten hits. The DRW are sitting at our usual table, nursing our ginger ales, trying to look nonchalant. The bar is full of guys. And none of them are high school guys. It's a nuclear fusion of foreign Y-chromosomes. And we're in the centre of it.

Every May, four groups of post-secondary students flow into town. Physics and engineering students compete from universities across the country for summer jobs at the plant, to conduct nuclear experiments that might land them author credits in scientific journals; co-op students vie for work term positions that might lead to an AECL job after graduation; forestry students from the University of Toronto arrive for a forestry boot camp to see what a forest really looks like; and hydro boys complete their hands-on nuclear power plant operator training up the road at the nuclear power demonstration station near Rolphton. The first clue the summer students have hit town is when the water tower changes itself to Beer River. The zenith of undergrad humour. And they're all men. Dozens of men. Dozens of men who have no idea nobody wants to go out with us. I'm sitting at the end of the table with my back to whoever's sitting behind us, watching the band, when Debbie elbows me in the ribs. "Don't look now, but someone from the table full of summer students is coming our way." I feel a tap on my right shoulder.

"Wanna dance?" new guy says. I nod, get up and wind my way to the dance floor. I have an ulterior motive. Or two, actually. If I dance close enough to the front of the band, maybe Tom will notice how popular I am. Fall-back position, the DRW will be the first to get to know the current crop of students. Win–win. New guy and I writhe to "Smoke on the Water," followed by "Knock Three Times," and "Rocket Man." The band takes a break. New guy and I clap and head back to our tables. "Do you and your friends want to join us?" he asks. "You can fill us in on what there is to do around here."

"Sure," I say. I rein in my feet and manage to walk super casually back to our table to tell the rest of the DRW to gather up their ginger ales. "Don't muck this up," I say. "This could be our ticket for the summer." I have no idea how not to muck things up.

We pull some extra chairs over to where the summer students are sitting. There are five guys and four of us. Good, there's a spare, I think. We won't have to divvy them up evenly. The new guys say they are national students, from as far away as Vancouver. Their names are Eric, Chris, Harry, Arthur and Fred. "So other than this place, where's the excitement?" says Eric, the guy who asked me to dance. I look sideways at Debbie, Ruth and Julie, trying to decide what to say that won't sound too small town. I run through the options in my head. There's the Byeways, of course. Will they get the wrong idea if I mention the strippers? The pizza at the Deep River Restaurant is definitely a big draw, and it would be especially good if they showed up when Ruth is on shift. And of course, the trip across the border to Quebec for high-test Brador beer and last call at three in the morning after the Byeways closes. The dairy for ice cream. But before I can begin my enumeration of the entertainment highlights, Julie pipes in.

"We have the beaches, the yacht and tennis club, the golf club, the cross-river swim, canoeing, sailing, water skiing, hiking in the bush and picnics at Indian Point on the Quebec side," Julie rhymes off. I look at her as if she's gone insane. She's making it sound like we're a summer camp!

"Fantastic," says Chris. "Sounds just like a summer camp! Only we're getting paid to be here! Who wants to play tennis tomorrow?" Julie and Chris discuss tennis court times, while my head spins. Ruth and Eric start talking about Vancouver, a place that's pretty much as far away as you can get from here. A place she dearly wants to go. Debbie learns that Harry is taking physics and asks him his opinion about whether or not girls can be quantum mechanics and whether or not it's like being a real mechanic. That leaves me with Fred and Arthur, who clear me in height by about two inches. Great. My two guys don't even add up to one I'd like to go out with. I wouldn't make Tom jealous dancing with either of them. Or even both of them at the same time. The band wraps up its final set and the waitress starts hovering to solicit for last call.

"Curfew's at midnight," says Ruth. "We gotta go." Nice play. Tell them we have a curfew. They probably already think we're as feeble as summer campers.

"Can we walk you girls home?" says Fred.

We head to the door just as the Ravens finish their last set. At least Tom will see me leaving with a bunch of guys. That's got to be worth something. "Where are we headed?" asks Chris.

"Just down the way on the highway a bit, towards the Catholic school," says Ruth. "Not far."

We walk along the edge of the highway east of Deep River Road and turn down a back alley just past the auto body shop. There are no street lights, but the moon is bright tonight. We pass the school and head to the door of the building beside it. Sisters of St. Joseph Convent, the sign says, clear as day under the full moon. Ruth takes a huge bunch of keys out of her massive purse and unlocks the outer door. "Thanks for a lovely evening," she says, as she ushers the rest of the DRW into the hushed convent.

The guys remain, dumbfounded, on the path in front of the doors, as Ruth ushers us inside. "Couldn't you just see it if they think we're nuns?" says Julie.

"We need to fix this now," I say.

Ruth swings the door back open. Luckily, the guys are still standing there, wondering what just happened. "Don't worry. We're not nuns. At least not yet. Debbie and I are just staying here for the summer," she says. "Long story. See you guys at tennis tomorrow. Right after church. Let me write down the convent phone number for you just in case."

The convent is a long, narrow two-story building. The front door leads to a small foyer that has one flight of stairs that goes up to the bedrooms and another that goes down to the pastoral reception room, chapel, and nuns' day quarters. It's as spare as a convent should be. The asbestos tile floors are yellow, and maybe that's the colour they are, or maybe they used to be beige before generations of floor wax intervened. The walls are painted with leftovers donated by the hospital, a vomitus green. There are no phones, except for the one in the phone booth that sits outside the communal living room, at end of the hall near the kitchen. It's a proper phone booth, with a glass door that folds inward, glass walls, and a black rotary phone that runs on nickels, dimes and quarters. The phone never rings except when there's an ecclesiastical emergency.

Debbie and Ruth's parents are not getting along, so Mrs. Dixon has taken the three younger girls out west to live with her sister. That's why the twins are staying at the convent. Despite its aesthetic challenges, the convent is an ideal clubhouse and the DRW have the run of the place. There's a combination TV, radio and record player housed in a walnut cabinet as big as a coffin. It was brand new in the 1950s. The room is chock full with brown Naugahyde lounge chairs, patched with silver duct tape where the stuffing threatens to escape. The nuns sit in them and rest their puffy feet, while they watch reruns of *Bewitched* and *I Dream of Jeanie*, as if the TV cannot bear to drag itself into the 1970s.

Sister Mary comes into the room as Debbie, Ruth, Julie and I are hanging out after school, and asks us about our day. "I don't care how much you guys like Mr. Wylie," I say. "I swear, after this year I'm never taking chemistry again. I am tired of losing my tights to hydrochloric acid." I'm only halfway through recounting my science wardrobe malfunction when the phone in the phone booth rings. Sister Mary clutches the wooden cross that hangs around her neck and hurries down the hall. We hear her answer the phone, and then there's silence while she listens to the person on the other end.

"I see," she says. "Just a moment." She comes back into the lounge, looks at us with her inscrutable nun's countenance, and says, "Arthur is on the line. He wants to know if you need a ride to Byeways tonight and do you want a ride to the Quebec side afterwards."

"Must be a wrong number," says Ruth. "We don't know an Arthur."

Sister Mary looks unconvinced but says, "I will give you girls the benefit of the doubt. As you know, we're all off on a Sisters of St. Joseph retreat down the Valley in Combermere on the weekend, so I will have to trust you to conduct yourselves like ladies. I'm going to bed now."

It's mid-June, the waning days of grade 12, and Debbie and Ruth turn eighteen two days from now. Drinking age, finally. I have another year and a quarter to go, which of course has not stood in my way so far. "You guys come over to the convent Saturday after the nuns leave. We'll cook a steak dinner for our birthday and then we'll go out to the Elms for our first legal drink," Debbie says.

Julie and I arrive at the convent on Saturday at six, bearing potatoes wrapped in foil and a chocolate cake from the A&P. Ruth's borrowed some records from the library: Simon and Garfunkel, Paul Simon solo, Carly Simon. All the Simons and Simon cohorts we're obsessed with at the moment. We load the vinyl platters on the stereo, on top of each other in a huge stack, and give the nuns' pristine HiFi a workout. We talk earnestly about our plans after we finish high school next year. Debbie wants to be a nurse. "The guidance counsellor says I shouldn't set my sights so high," she says. "I'll probably be a waitress at Jordie's forever."

Julie is thinking about hotel and food management. "Couldn't you just see it if I end up running Maxim's restaurant in Paris? Do you think you need to know French for that? Maybe I should start taking French." My sights are still set on actress or figure skater, or in a pinch, ballet dancer.

"If we're going to have steak, we should have red wine, especially now that we're officially grown-ups," Debbie says. "I accidently saw some in the sacristy the other day." I know nothing about convents or nuns or sacristies, but I follow her down the hall to the chapel, and sure enough, there are two cases of California Muscatel wine on the floor of the little room where the priest gets ready for chapel service. "It's supposed to be for communion but I don't think this is officially the blood of Jesus yet," Debbie says. Blood? Jesus? Blood of freaking Jesus? All we have at the United Church is grape juice from the A&P. And only at Christmas and Easter. I didn't know Catholics were so out there. No way I'm drinking blood. Debbie rummages in the little drawers that keep the priest's accoutrements for mass and then lifts her hand above her head triumphantly, brandishing a t-shaped corkscrew with a brass handle. "Jackpot," she says. "I think we'll need two bottles, at least."

I trail Debbie back to the lounge, where she rounds up four goblets that look like they were sent from central casting to stand in for the Holy Grail, and pours the wine. "I never really knew what wine tasted like before, but this is delicious," says Ruth. "The potatoes are in the oven and they're going to take a while. Anyone want more wine?" We are well into the second bottle when Ruth starts cooking the steak. When it's ready, she divides it among four plates and we carry our dinner out to the lounge.

"Ruth, how come you hogged the whole tenderloin bit?" says Debbie. "It's both our birthdays. You should share!"

Ruth ignores her. "Here's more wine, everyone. This is the best birthday ever." She takes another gulp from her glass and leans back in the lounger, plate full of steak on her lap. "You know, I understand now why people drink wine at the DRR. It really makes the food taste better. Anyone else want more?" Ruth proceeds to perfect her wine appreciation. "That was good steak, but I must have eaten too much. Suddenly I don't feel well." She gets up, lurches towards the bathroom and almost makes it there before she barfs up a grape-infused mix of steak and potato down the front of her new, white, Indian cotton gauze top. It flows down to her shoes and oozes on to the yellow floor. "Why is the room spinning? I have to go to bed." She crawls into the bathroom and curls up on the floor.

"She barfed up the best bit of the steak!" says Debbie. "And now I'm going to spend the rest of my birthday cleaning up her mess." She huffs off to find the mop.

Meanwhile, I scamper down the hall to the phone booth, fish a dime out of my pocket, and dial the hall phone for

Maple Lodge, the residence where Arthur and Fred are staying. It rings and rings and rings and rings until someone picks up. "Mario's Pizza," Arthur says.

"Stop being a jerk," I say. "I'm at the convent and need to be picked up right now. Ruth just puked up Jesus." I let Debbie and Julie figure out how to drag Ruth upstairs to her nun's cell and get everything shipshape for when Sister Mary and the crew get back tomorrow. I'm not wrecking my Saturday night for dead Jesus, who is somehow alive and then dead again in a pool of regurgitated wine.

25

Constellations

Angela's hanging out with Fred this summer. Keith bit the dust once he left to go to fireman college. Fred and some of the other students at the plant have rented a huge aluminum canoe for the duration. We call it the super-canoe. It fits at least six people and with six paddles it goes pretty fast. The super-canoe lives in the bush just beside the motorboat launch ramp. It's a good thing it fits six people, because it takes about six people to heft it into the water. Nobody is too worried the super-canoe will go missing from its bush hangout, but just in case, everyone keeps their paddles at home. The summer students have pristine paddles, with gleaming lacquer and red racing stripes where the handle meets the shaft. Like every kid in town, I already own a canoe paddle, only mine is bashed up and the finish is peeling off like sheets of skin after a bad sunburn. Paddles are pretty much issued at birth, along with a set of skate guards and brown rubber winter galoshes. Everything you need to survive.

I've had enough of the beach for the day, so I'm on my ancient, rusty, CCM glider bike heading out from the parking lot, when I run into Angela and Fred on their way for a swim after work. "Hey," Angela says. "We're going to take the canoe across the river after dinner tonight and we need at least two more people. Wanna come?"

At quarter to seven, I retrieve my paddle from the garage and balance it awkwardly over my handle bars to cycle down to the river. "Going out," I shout over my shoulder, vaguely towards the direction of my house. I meet up with Angela and Fred at the boat launch, along with Arthur, who's been rounded up to be our fourth. I ditch my bike in the underbrush and use all of my eighty-five-pound body mass to help turn the canoe over. We drag it into position at the bottom of the ramp, pushing it forward until it's completely in the water. I chuck my sandals, towel and paddle into the canoe, wade into the water, and jump in mid-boat. The canoe bottoms out on the vestiges of asphalt where the ramp dissolves into the water. "Better take off our watches or they'll get wet," Arthur says, "I'll put them in my car." Fred and Arthur manage to successfully complete our launch and we aim the canoe due north, towards the other side of the river and Indian Point Beach, a swath of pristine sand on the uninhabited Quebec side that's outfitted with firepits and picnic tables by the Deep River Motorboat Club. No drinking water except the river. No outhouses except the bush. No lights except the stars. And at most times, more bears than people.

Angela and I kneel in the fat part of the boat, each taking one side, knees on top of floater cushions. We don't bother with lifejackets, because the bulky orange slabs get in the way of proper paddle strokes. The aluminum gunnels are so high I can't kneel with my butt on top of my feet if I want to reach my paddle over the side, so instead I sit tall on my thin shins, which even at the start of this journey are beginning to whine about when it will end. I hear a distant rumble and the sky to the west starts to shimmer with what looks like wisps of electric green clouds. It's not thunder, though. "Wow," says Fred. "Northern lights! They make a noise? Better than those lame psychedelic lights at the Elms." Same old, same old, I think. You can see them most nights in August, if you pay attention.

We land at Indian Point Beach in the twilight and pull the canoe up on the sand. The only light is a sliver of moon on the horizon and the reflection of the darkening sky on the water. Fred and Arthur gather twigs from the bush at the edge of the sand and start a campfire. Angela throws a can of Mountain Dew in my direction, which sprays sticky lemon-lime fizz in my face when I open it. Unlike me, I hope bears can resist Mountain Dew. I spread out my towel and lie on my back to see the stars. Orion's belt is just starting to emerge: Alnitak, Alnilam and Mintaka forming a straight row across the hunter's midsection. And on and on, until every square inch of sky is pinpoints of light, set against the luminous veil of the Milky Way.

"Hey! That's a satellite. Is it spying on us? Did you see it stall there, just above where the plant is?" says Angela. One small dot is moving counter-clockwise through the stratosphere with a syncopated rhythm, weaving slightly like it's trying to navigate around errant stars in its path. We watch until it goes past the horizon on towards the southern hemisphere. My brother has a telescope at home. He says that spy satellites take photos of what's happening on earth, then eject the film, attached to little parachutes that get scooped up mid-air by spy planes. Probably James Bond intercepts them up, teeter-tottering on the wing, then jumping off before hurtling down thousands of feet before firing up the jetpack on his back. My brother says it takes about an hour and a half for a satellite to complete one circuit of Earth. I imagine an eight-lane highway with 1,000 autonomous-car satellites spread out in lines in space, wrapping themselves endlessly around the circumference of the planet. Electronic shutters whirring non-stop.

It's pitch black outside of the ring of light thrown by the fire. "Let's sing something," I say. We argue about what to sing. "Rocket Man?" "Smoke on the Water?" "Wild Horses?" "I'm so sick of 'Rocket Man,'" says Arthur. "And if I hear 'Smoke on the Water' one more time I'll puke. I swear that jukebox at the Byeways only has two songs on it." We settle on campfire favourites: "Kumbaya," "Michael Row the Boat Ashore," "Don't Throw Your Junk in My Backyard." I know the campfire favourites, because even kids who grew up in Deep River go to camp. I've been to Camp Lau-Ren. Apparently, a camp is not a camp until it has a name with a hyphen in it. Camp Lau-Ren is a church summer camp six miles up the road from town. I went there for a week one summer with all the girls from the junior choir, plus some kids from down the valley. Eganville. Killaloe. Cobden. We swam in the same river where we got our swimming badges, tanned on the same sand we have at Lamure Beach, crashed about in the same boreal forest in my backyard, and climbed on the same ice age granite as Rabbit Rock across the street from my house. Camp was an eye-opener, for sure.

Fred and Arthur will finish their work terms and head back to campus at Waterloo in a couple of weeks. "Come on, guys," I say. "Please tell us what goes on at that plant! We live here and we don't even know!"

"We could tell you, but then we'd have to kill you," says Arthur, and then he makes "doo doo doo doo, doo doo doo

doo" *Twilight Zone* sounds. "Can't be as pathetic as your summer jobs."

Angela's working at Ryan's Campsite Gift Shop and Gas Bar, on the highway almost all the way to the Byeways. She looks after the cash register in the gift shop and also pumps the gas. "You would not believe it," she says. "The number of customers who will not let me pump the gas because I'm a girl. They don't even know how to work the pump and they still won't even let me undo their gas caps. Mr. Ryan has to come out and calm them down. On the plus side, they usually give me a tip. Sometimes two bucks. Like I'm a waitress or something."

"Or a Byeways stripper," says Fred.

Angela is not impressed. "I'd be willing to bet I get better tips from Ryan's," she says. As if this is a contest she even wants to enter, let alone win.

"Well at least I only work at the playground from nine to noon," I say. "That's the upside. The downside is Mr. Evraire is insane and I never know what I'm supposed to be doing from day to day."

"You should try working with sub-atomic particles like I do," says Arthur. "Mr. Evraire would be a picnic after that."

"Picnics. Don't get me started on picnics. Or breakfast hikes. Wait. What time do you think it is?" I say. "I think it's way late." Nobody knows. But the fire's dying anyhow, so we decide to head home. Fred holds the flashlight as we wrestle the canoe back into the water, just as thick fog starts to roll in. It's the time of year when the air temperature starts to be colder than the water. Angela and I fling our water buffalo sandals over the gunnel and jump in, just as the canoe clears the twenty-foot drop off and just as Fred's pristine paddle slides off the seat into the depths. Crap. I take one for the team and pass my extremely experienced paddle to the front.

The fog obliterates anything beyond the end of our paddles. Fred's flashlight does nothing except bounce the beam back into our eyes. Except then it does do something: flicker then fade out completely.

"Well, we know we came pretty much straight across," says Fred, "So if we just head towards the opposite shore in the same direction the back of the canoe is pointed, we should be fine. Although I wish I had my slide rule. I could triangulate the speed of the current with the width of the river and the lights on the other side. That is, if we could see lights on the other side. Never mind." Three paddles dip into the water to propel us towards what we hope is our side of the river, close to town.

"So how long should this take?" I ask.

"Took us about half an hour on the way over, I think." says Fred. "With four paddles."

"Okay. How about this?" I say. "The full version of 'American Pie' is eight minutes long and I know all the words. If we sing the whole thing five times, we should be almost at the other shore by then. If we aren't, we'll know something's wrong." I tell everyone to repeat after me as I recite the lyrics. After we've sung the song for the fiftieth time, we start to see lights from the town ghosting through the fog. Or at least we hope it's the town. The right town. On second thought, given its obsession with dying, "American Pie" was probably not the best choice. Maybe "The Sound of Silence" would have been a smarter idea. Darkness and friends and all that. Too late.

If we miss our mark to the west, we could end up at Pine Point Beach or even Camp Lau-Ren. If we miss it to the east, we have a bit more to worry about, because there aren't too many sandy landings unless we hit the plant, which means even more to worry about, except for the fact that search lights would illuminate our arrival and sirens would welcome us to shore, without the welcome part.

Instead of worse possibilities, we end up at Pumphouse Park, a five-minute walk from the boat launch. Close enough to claim success, anyhow. We leave the canoe pulled up at the rocky Pumphouse shore and walk down towards the yacht club carrying our paddles, underneath streetlights buzzing with moths and flies. "I'll drive all you guys home," says Arthur. I leave my bike to collect for tomorrow, except I think it's already tomorrow. The dashboard clock in Arthur's Datsun says 04:00. This is not good.

Arthur drives east along Beach Road and up LaSalle to Angela's house. "I'll get out here too," I say. The Datsun's doors are heavier than a full refrigerator. No need to slam a car door in front of my house as well. I head home around the curve of Darwin Crescent, walk up the driveway and lift the garage door to put my paddle away. It takes a nanosecond before I realize this is not a good idea. The metal hinges creak to announce their lack of maintenance, the porch light goes on and my mother appears on the step in her pink floral summer housecoat that zips up the front.

"It's four in the morning! Where the heck were you! Were you out with Angela? Her mother called me five hours ago. You are in such trouble."

I slither upstairs to bed, muttering under my breath, "We didn't do anything wrong. We didn't have a watch. We saw the northern lights and a satellite and the Milky Way, and sang around the campfire, and a porcupine scared the boys, and we canoed through the fog, and it will only be this summer once. Isn't that what you sent me to camp to do a few years ago?"

Despite my truncated night, I still manage to get up in time to skulk out of the house just after sunrise to avoid my mother's wrath. I retrieve my bike from the bush at the boat launch and head off to Cedar Park. I tell Liz it's been a long night and set her free to conduct an art extravaganza. No baseball today. I snooze in the supply shed, while Liz organizes a macramé marathon. Bracelets and plant hangers for everyone and their mothers. And even an extra for Mr. Evraire. And his mother. Just in case he ever shows up.

After playground, I sequester myself at the beach for the afternoon, eating grape Popsicles and reading *A Wrinkle in Time* until Angela shows up after she's done at Ryan's. "I'm not allowed to hang out with you anymore," she says. "My mother thinks you are a bad influence." She laughs. "She doesn't even think Fred is a bad influence for taking us out in the canoe after dark! You are a badass!" Angela's a year ahead of me and she's starting at Western to be a teacher in September, so I'll hardly see her anymore anyway. She'll find a new boyfriend and probably never come back. Why does she want to be a teacher? That's the last thing I'd want to be. Like being a playground leader only worse. You actually have to pay attention to the kids and there's probably no shed to nap in. I think I'll stick with famous actress. I'm stuck here for an entire other year. Both her mother and my mother are mad at me and mad at each other and who knows who else is mad at me. Probably Mr. Evraire. And Mr. Fraser. And Mr. Morris. And for sure, Mr. Smith and likely Mr. Wilson too. Take a number and get in line, I think.

Fred and Arthur arrive at the beach a little while later and swim out to second raft, where Angela and I are sitting with our feet dangling in late August water that's rapidly heading towards un-swimmable. "Wanna buy my bike for five bucks?" says Fred. "Don't want to bother taking it back with me." He bought it from Canadian Tire on the highway in May. It's almost brand new.

"Sure, if you want," I say, with my quasi-disinterested outside voice, while my inside voice says: "Three speeds! Wow. I've never had speeds. And handbrakes. And blue. And a crossbar. And everything. Coaster brakes, you are history!" I name my new bike Fred. Fred and I will go places. You'll see.

26

Take a Letter

Grade 9 typing turned out to be a gateway drug. My elective slots are otherwise engaged, so I continue my typing education in night school, while still a full-time student in day school. Turns out I'm a whiz at typing, and it's always good for girls to have something to fall back on. Or at least, that's what Mr. Foster, the guidance counsellor, says. He seems a little doubtful the whole acting thing is going to pan out. I do have a plan, though. If I don't get to be a famous actress, I'll just switch to figure skating or ballet.

In night school, we have electric typewriters and the focus is on speed and accuracy. Words per minute do not count if they're not really words or not the words they were meant to be. Electric typewriters up the speed quotient significantly, which is not always good because electric typewriters are as twitchy as wild horses. Just hovering your fingers in the general vicinity of the keyboard can cause the typewriter to bolt into action, spewing gibberish across the page. But to give Mr. Wilson his touch-typing-teaching due, my hands operate with disembodied efficiency to move words directly from my eyes or ears to the typed page.

By the summer I graduate from high school, and I have a certificate that says I type 120 accurate words per minute, and I have also mastered "Pitman Script," a form of shorthand that combines symbols with alphabet letters. I now have a full roster of skills to fall back on if famous actress and world champion figure skater remain off the table. And these are exactly the skills that get me a summer job at the plant. Or more correctly, the exact skills that allow my dad to pull the strings required to get me a summer job at the plant. At last, I think, I'll finally learn what goes on there.

I ride to work with my dad and Mr. Ross, who carpool. There is still a bus, but hardly anyone rides it anymore except shift workers who want to sleep on the way there or the way home. Gas stations now dot the highway at semi-regular intervals, and the road is paved all the way to the plant gate, so no reason not to drive a car. Nobody brings lunch though, because the cafeteria remains in full swing, red Jell-O and all. My job is junior secretary and file clerk at the personnel office, filling in for the regular secretarial staff as they take summer vacation. Mr. Brant, the head of personnel, is my boss. He golfs with my dad. I'd better not mess this up. The personnel office is just inside the plant gate, beside the main parking lot, where my dad drops me off. He has his own parking spot outside the Nuclear Materials Control building where he works. He waves as he continues beyond another gate and into the plant's nether regions. I have an actual job at the actual plant and I'm still not allowed to see what actually goes on here.

I arrive at my first day of work in a lime green, puffed-sleeve minidress I made myself and well-worn-in water buffalo sandals, because I have never had any need for any other summer footwear. Mrs. Lafontaine, the senior secretary, meets me at the personnel office door and ushers me into the break room for a little "welcome aboard" lecture. The break room is in the back corner of the office, equipped with two couches that have seen many ample behinds, a side table littered with *Scientific American, Bulletin of the Atomic Scientists* and *Physics Weekly*, and a coffee percolator. Mrs. Lafontaine firmly closes the door. "There's a few things you need to know about our office. Mr. Brant does not like bare legs, so please wear nylons." Okay. I'm thinking that means pants or shorts are also completely out of the question, even though shorts would be longer than my dress. Also, I think wearing nylons with water buffalo sandals is anatomically impossible, given the loop that goes over the big toe. This might be a problem. "You should know that Mr. Brant likes his coffee with two creams and two sugars, the first one at 9:15, then one at 10:15, but not in the break room, that's where the rest of us take our break, and one at 2:15, unless he decides he wants one at 3:45, and maybe at 4:00, but not usually." Mrs. Lafontaine is gifting me with what she says is the most important job of the secretarial pool: making Mr. Brant's coffee. I do not drink coffee and do not know how to make coffee. Mr. Brant may be in for an unwelcome surprise.

Mrs. Lafontaine shows me to my desk. All the "girls" in the personnel office sit at desks in an open room lined with filing cabinets. According to Mrs. Lafontaine, I'll be moving around depending on who's on vacation that particular week. "Don't get too comfortable," she says. I'm guessing she means this literally. The men's offices are located around three sides of the building, hiding the windows from everyone else's view behind doors with frosted windows etched with the name of the occupant. The doors are always closed. This is actually a boon to the inhabitants outside the doors: Mrs. Lafontaine and Miss Brum treat our outer-sanctum like the waiting room of a beauty salon, with stacks of *True Confessions* and *National Enquirer* magazines in their desk drawers, and petty cash boxes turned into makeshift makeup kits. Usually, two of the secretaries are camped out in the breakroom, teasing each other's hair and bobby-pinning the bits in front of their ears into spit curls. Mr. Brant never gives any sign he notices either these desk-absences or the modifications of appearance. I'm beginning to think it's Mrs. Lafontaine that doesn't like bare legs, because obviously Mr. Brant is oblivious.

It does not take me long to discover that being a secretary is mostly filing files, retrieving files and twiddling my thumbs awaiting the call from Mr. Brant that he has a need for my services to "take a letter." The most exciting part of my day is attending to Mr. Brant's important correspondence. His dictation usually goes something like this: "Dear Mister Smith semicolon We have received your application for the position of nuclear rocket scientist period Thank you for your application period new paragraph We will review your credentials after the close of the competition on July fifteenth period We thank you for your interest period If you are not selected for an interview comma we will keep your resume on file for six months period closing salutation Yours sincerely comma Mister Fred Brant." After I have recorded this dictation in my steno pad, I read it back to him to make sure I have captured it correctly, and so that Mr. Brant has an opportunity to fine-tune his eloquent prose before I type it up.

A version of this happens about three times a week. I don't know what else Mr. Brant does with his time, since us "girls" open all the letters that arrive, read them and summarize any actions required, file them, create new file folders if necessary, get all the letters that are going out ready for the mailman, fix the typewriters if they need fixing, order the office supplies, receive the office supplies, put the office supplies away, make the coffee for coffee break, circulate the birthday cards, and empty Mr. Brant's ashtray.

After a few weeks of the dictation routine, I start to wonder if I'm missing something. Doesn't it take more time for Mr. Brant to dictate the letter than to write it down himself and hand it to me to type? Since there are only about three different variations of letter — we got your application, we'd like to interview you, you didn't get the job — why doesn't Mr. Brant simply tell me to copy variation A, B or C, and insert the relevant applicant details? Why does he assume that, although I know how to record and type English sentences, I don't have a firm grasp of punctuation or the basic structure of a letter? And how is it possible that a seventeen-year-old who has a high school diploma with wet ink can easily, with ample time to twiddle thumbs, complete all the tasks required for a job most of the secretaries have held for twenty years? I decide that maybe things need a little shaking up.

I knock on Mr. Brant's door and he bids me to enter. He's reading the newspaper with his feet on the desk. "You are just in time," he says. "This ashtray is full." Then he returns to the sports section and waves me out of the room. I pick up the ashtray and back out of the office. Maybe shaking things up is not a good idea. He seems to know what it takes to run this office. Best to just go with the flow. But maybe I can decide what that flow looks like.

The next time Mr. Brant summons me to take dictation, I ask him what type of letter it is. "Just curious," I say. "I want

to get better at learning how things are done around here."
He looks up and seems to admire my summer student
initiative. Or I think that's what his look means. Mr. Brant
has never spoken a single word to me that doesn't involve
letter content, coffee requirements or full ashtrays. "It's an
applicant," he says. I flip to the page in my steno pad where
I've already Pittman'd this version of the letter, and pretend
to record it in shorthand. I didn't take shorthand because I
liked it. I only took it so Angela and I could pass secret notes
in class and encrypt our diaries. Shorthand is a pain because
I have to remember which slanted line means "d," and which
one means "n," and which one means "p." If I mess it up, I
spend more time trying to transcribe my dictation than
taking it down in the first place. Also, it freaks me out that
Mr. Brant always gives me an oral test on the accuracy of my
shorthand. Probably because he wants to torment me. Either
that, or he has nothing else to do.

The next time there's not too much of anything to do,
which is immediately when I get back to my desk, I pre-type
five copies each of the three kinds of letters, leaving out the
address and the date, then deftly file them in my desk drawer.
Unfortunately, this does not achieve the outcome I'm aiming
for, since it leaves me with even more idle time on my hands.
Not only am I not transcribing shorthand, I don't even have
to spend much time typing the letters. The *National Enquirer*
is not quite my thing, so I start bringing a book to work,
hiding it under a file folder or in my top desk drawer. I don't
know why I'm trying so hard to hide it. Clearly Mr. Brant will
never notice. While I'm waiting for something to do, I read a
dog-eared copy of *Valley of the Dolls*, which turns out not to
be about dolls at all, interspersed with an equally dog-eared
copy of *A Wrinkle in Time*. Meanwhile, I could have been at

the beach doing the exact same thing, instead of having summer proceed without me outside the windows I can't see.

During the course of the summer, I fill in for Miss Brum's job, Miss Kelly's job and Mrs. Patterson's job, all of which involve filing, typing and re-filing. Then it's time for Mrs. Lafontaine to go on three weeks' vacation. She has the most seniority so she's allowed to take three weeks in a row. She tells me I will have to fill in for her because some of her tasks are not in the other girls' job descriptions. "They aren't allowed to do some of these things," she says. "The union will not allow it." Seems like sound logic to me. I'm game. Especially if it gets me out of Mr. Brant's letters. For the next three weeks I will be in charge of processing new employees. As she runs out the door on Friday afternoon to start her vacation, Mrs. Lafontaine points me in the direction of the binder that holds the standard operating procedures for new employees. "Just study up on how to add them to payroll, how to enroll them in benefits and how to issue a dosimeter," she instructs.

I try to look very official as I smuggle the binder home for the weekend, even though it has a big sticker that says "Confidential. Do Not Remove." smack dab on the front. In red. The binder instructions turn out to be pretty straight forward. No wonder Mrs. Lafontaine doesn't want anyone else to know what she does. There are routine forms to fill out and type. But the dosimeters! They need to be collected from the occupational safety office. Inside the second gate. Jackpot. I will finally get close to the nuclear action, whatever it is. It's probably just like that *Twilight Zone* episode where interstellar spaceships are stored on the grounds of the nuclear plant. That's why nobody's allowed to see what's there and why my dad is sworn to secrecy.

I go into work on Monday and sit at Mrs. Lafontaine's desk, thumbing through the latest scandals in the *National Enquirer*, while I wait for all the new hires to arrive. Nobody shows up. None on Tuesday. None on Wednesday. None on Thursday. None on Friday. I'm almost finished *Valley of the Dolls* and still no dolls have shown up either. On to *Airport*. I've never been to an airport, this better be good. Hopefully no bait and switch this time. The three weeks tick by as slowly as a clock in the math classroom, without any sign of new employees. Mrs. Lafontaine returns from vacation, and suddenly it's my last day of work before I go off to university. At 10:15, there's a card waiting for me in the break room. And a cake. And Mr. Brant. He makes a short farewell speech. "Thank you for your fine work this summer. I'll be sure to tell your father how well you did. Come back and work here any time." Good luck with that, Mr. Brant. I'm outta here. To Waterloo. To eventually get a job that doesn't involve making coffee for men.

27

Nothing like This Place

It's October but it hasn't even snowed yet in Waterloo, Ontario. Just rained non-stop. That's why we call it the Waterversity of Uniloo. Ruth and I are here at school, but Debbie's at McMaster and Julie's at Guelph. Because it specializes in science, technology, engineering and math, Waterloo's male/female ratio is thirteen to one. Which is the main reason I chose it, plus the fact that lots of kids from our school are here as well, but for things like science, technology, engineering and math. Not arts like I'm taking. I don't like any of my allotted thirteen guys, though. And neither does Ruth.

Ruth's in the south quad of the Village Two residence and I'm in the east. I always walk over and pick her up for breakfast, because otherwise she'd sleep through our eight-thirty philosophy class. Plus, I hate going into the dining hall by myself because it freaks me out. There are more people in this dining hall than in my high school and I know none of them. None of them care who I am or who my parents are or what they do or even if I have parents. Awesome. Creepy.

At the dining hall, I grab my meal ticket out of the holder on the wall and hand it to the meal ticket lady. It's a piece of cardboard in a plastic sleeve that has my Polaroid headshot on it. In my meal ticket photo, I have a scarf covering my head, tied tightly at the back of my neck to corral any rogue unwashed hairs. The meal ticket lady does not need to spend much time comparing me to my photo, because this is what I look like most days. Hair washing is a limited commodity. We have communal bathing facilities and it's a major scheduling issue to get myself out of bed to line up for the shower in the bathroom in time to dry my hair before heading over to coerce Ruth out of bed and into the bathroom in time to get her hair dry in time to get to breakfast in time to get to our first class. So, the solution is I just don't wash my hair. I have scarves that match every outfit in my closet, which is not too hard because all I ever wear is faded blue, elephant leg, Howick jeans and pastel-coloured Indian cotton gauze shirts, which chronically smell like patchouli from the Indian cotton gauze shirt store and Coty Wild Musk. We apply it with abandon, because once it's on our wrists we acquire olfactory paralysis. We all steep in it, oily, unctuous, male pheromone inciting. We hope.

Ruth and I walk to class along the path that winds from Village Two to Village One to the Arts building, dodging goose poop and mud puddles, discussing Kant and Wittgenstein. "I'm extra tired today," says Ruth. "The guys on the floor downstairs were showing *Deep Throat* outside in the quad. On the building. Just below my window. At two in the morning."

"Was it any good?" I say.

"Couldn't tell," says Ruth. "I couldn't really see it. The guys seemed to like it, though."

"Whereof one cannot speak, one must be silent," I say. "Wittgenstein."

"What can be shown cannot be said," Ruth says. "Wittgenstein."

"What we cannot speak about, we must pass over in silence," I say. "Wittgenstein."

"If people never did silly things, nothing intelligent would ever get done," Ruth says. "Wittgenstein." He's got that right. I hope that's on the midterm.

* * *

The bus ride home for Thanksgiving is actually three buses. The first one, a Greyhound from Waterloo to Toronto, takes three hours to complete its leisurely path through southern Ontario farmland. I look out the window at cows standing in the rain on grass that's still green. I'm reading Rainer Maria Rilke, *Letters to a Young Poet*, except it's in German so the cover says *Briefe an einen jungen Dichter*. I mostly just hold the book in my lap, like I've just set it down for a moment to rest my eyes, so anyone who looks can see I'm reading in German. My pretentions know no bounds. Ruth's choice for impressing bus passengers is Kant's *Prolegomena to Any Future Metaphysics*. "This is interesting," she says. "Thoughts without content are empty, intuitions without concepts are blind. Kant is so profound! What did we do before we knew Kant existed?" Almost all the subjects I'm taking I never knew existed. Philosophy. Sociology. Political science. Computer programming. My brain hurts.

Our second bus goes all the way to Pembroke, but not until we've cooled our heels in Toronto for two hours. The bus station is right downtown and looks like it was an exciting place to be when it was built in the 1930s, before the terrazzo floors got smudged black with discarded gum and the comfortable chairs were replaced with molded orange plastic seats with no backs, scarred with cigarette burns. The waiting room is not a place anyone wants to wait. Instead, Ruth and I kill time by going across the street to get Chinese food.

The Kwong Chow restaurant is on the second floor of a short brick building that's seen more of life than it wished it had. We go up a stairway lined with peeling red velvet wallpaper embossed with golden fans. The stair treads are shiny and concave from all the feet that have previously beaten a path to chow mien. I've never been here before. I've never even had Chinese food before. Ruth knows Kwong Chow because she's eaten here with her aunt who lives in the Toronto suburbs. "It's really, really, fancy," she says, "tablecloths and everything."

An Asian man wearing a grey suit vest and black bow tie ushers us to a table beside the dusty window, and a waiter hands us huge menus encased in red vinyl with a gold tassel on the spine, which are only slightly sticky from previous patrons' culinary adventures. There are posters on the walls advertising specialties of the house in Chinese script and, inexplicably, black and white photos of movie stars from thirty years ago. There are indeed tablecloths, but on top of the tablecloths are the exact same scalloped-edge paper placemats highlighting fancy mixed drinks as we have at the Deep River Restaurant. Only here, there are people actually drinking them. So that's what a Singapore Sling looks like in real life. The cherries really are that red. I want one of those little umbrellas. "Let's get one," I say. "We can share."

We pile our grubby yellow ripstop nylon knapsacks on the extra chairs. The knapsacks' claim to fame is that they fold away into a little pocket when you aren't using them, but once you liberate them from their pocket and open the drawstring at the top, they expand exponentially into mini duffle bags. Their tragic flaw is when you stuff the knapsack to bursting, you can see right through the yellow exterior, so my pink underwear is on full display. Good thing nobody knows me.

"I always get the dinner for one for one," Ruth says. "Or you can get the dinner for two for one, or the dinner for three for one. But not the dinner for four for one. I don't know why." The dinner for one has an eggroll, sweet and sour chicken balls and mixed vegetables. The mixed vegetables are canned peas and diced carrots. Maybe I have had Chinese food before and didn't know it.

* * *

The door on the bus to Pembroke wheezes open and greets us with an infusion of tobacco mixed with eau de road salt. Ruth and I each grab our own two seats in the middle. Not so close to the front that someone would quickly notice an empty seat and be tempted to sit beside us, and not too far towards the back to have to experience the smell of the bathroom ripening over the next seven hours. The bus chugs past high rises, low rises and industrial lands until we finally leave the urban sprawl that clings to Lake Ontario behind when we turn north off the highway towards Peterborough. It starts to sleet and the windshield wiper metronome squeaks as it keeps time with the weather. We stop for twenty minutes in Peterborough, enough time to use the land-based bathroom and drink rusty water reeking of chlorine from the fountain that loses pressure every time someone flushes. Only four hours left to go. Rilke isn't turning out to be as exciting as I thought. I buy a *Cosmopolitan* magazine at the newsstand. "How to Tell if You're Dateable: Take Our Quiz," it says on the cover. Territory Wittgenstein is certainly not going to address any time soon, even if he wasn't dead. I do not take the quiz. No need to prove the obvious.

We head on north, through Lakefield, Young's Point, Bancroft, Bird's Creek, Maynooth, Combermere, Barry's Bay, Wilno, Killaloe, Golden Lake, Eganville, Shady Nook. North and norther towards the Valley. It's snowing now. Big, wet flakes that slap against the bus windows and slide down to the sill where they pile up in the corner. "By the gar, when youse get to Shady Nook ya know youse er close to home," says a guy at the back of the bus. Clearly and proudly a local. "Any youse young lads got smokes left?" he asks the bus in general. I dearly hope not. I've already smoked a pack vicariously.

Pembroke's the end of the line for the Greyhound bus. To get all the way home, we need to wait another hour or two for the westbound Voyageur bus that heads towards North Bay, and then eventually goes all the way to Vancouver. The bus even says Vancouver on the front. Ruth and I share some fries from the chip truck that's clearing out its dregs before packing up for the night. Half price. We sit on the curb on top of our knapsacks, which are busy enhancing their grubbiness. I can see my breath. We left Waterloo this morning at eight and it will be close to midnight before we get to town. "Why on earth are you even bothering to come here? Your brother's not even coming home for Thanksgiving weekend. There's a curling bonspiel in North Bay. I'm too busy to make turkey, you know. You'll have to get pizza or something," my mother said, when I told her we'd be on the Friday night bus.

We're coming home because it's the only way to prove we've really left. A man will be imprisoned in a room with a door that's unlocked and opens inwards; as long as it does not occur to him to pull rather than push, says Wittgenstein.

I have a yellowing print that sports the sepia rainbow colour of decaying Kodak point-and-shoot photos, which shows four girls, young women really, standing at the top of a ridge against a background of Jack pines, red maples and yellow poplars. Our arms are linked. We're decked out in classic examples of 1974 fashion. A green, tweedy, belted, sweater-coat with a contrasting shawl collar in burnt orange. A jean jacket, crisp and blue. A nubby beige cable-knit sweater. A yellow cotton anorak with a drawstring at the waist. We stand with our backs to the Laurentian Mountains and the Ottawa River and the wilderness that goes on forever until you hit James Bay. I look squarely into the camera, willing my future to come into sharper focus. I know it's out there somewhere. Somewhere that's nowhere like this place.

Author's Note

In a feature piece about Deep River he wrote for *Maclean's* magazine in 1958, Peter C. Newman described it as "a suburb without a city." He went on to say, "the Utopian town where our atomic scientists live and play has no crime, no slums, no unemployment, and few mothers-in-law. But maybe you wouldn't like it after all." What could be more bizarre than a planned town plopped down fully formed in the middle of nowhere, inhabited by white-bread nuclear scientists and their nuclear families? They say everyone believes their family is normal, because that's the only version of normal they know. The same was true about growing up in the Petri dish that was Deep River in the 1960s and '70s. We had no idea how weird it was, nor how weird it might appear to those who had the misfortune not to grow up there. I wrote *Nowhere like This Place: Tales from a Nuclear Childhood* to both preserve and reveal that world. Despite its isolation, Deep River is the geographic equivalent of Six Degrees of Kevin Bacon. Everyone seems to know someone, or knows someone who knows someone, or knows someone who knows someone who knows someone with a connection to the town.

I have changed some names and identifying characteristics — probably for naught, because anyone who lived in town at the time would be able to figure it out and will probably waste a ridiculous amount of time doing so. In particular, I have changed some teachers' names, mostly because I can't remember them, and anyhow, their names are irrelevant to the story. The names of playmates and schoolmates, other than major characters, are sometimes randomly assigned because I can't recall exactly who I was hanging around with on any particular day.

Memory provides the entrails that go into the memoir sausage, and sausage-making can get messy. I am lucky to have a memory like a steel trap, but that doesn't mean my memory is infallible. Anyone who says writing a memoir is easy, because it all just comes out of your head, has never written a memoir. Or at least has never written a memoir that's doing its best to be factually correct. There are all kinds of historical facts that had the nerve to brazenly insert themselves into my story. I relied on library and internet research to verify facts about 1960s and '70s music, fashion and pop culture details, such as those related to Expo 67 in Chapter 9. I have not provided the complete list of sources I consulted for facts about Deep River and AECL, but trust me they were numerous and included, for example, *Deep River, 1945–1995*, a pictorial history of the town and its citizens, compiled by Joan Melvin in 1992 for the fiftieth anniversary of the town; the Peter C. Newman article noted above; and *The Early Years of Nuclear Energy Research in Canada* by George C. Laurence, who directed the staff that did the preparatory research, development and conceptual design of the Chalk River NRU reactor. If you suffer from severe insomnia, I'd be happy to lend it to you.

No, I did not carry a tape recorder around with me at all times when I was a kid, so of course the dialogue depicted here is not word-for-word what was actually said, but rather the essence of what I remember being said. Keen eyes will notice that several incidents I recount involve things that are, at best, ill-advised and, at worst, illegal. I recount them with the confidence that nobody is going to bother tracking down the owners of a dive bar that burned down thirty years ago.

When I visited the town at the end of April 2019, the snowbanks by the side of the road looked like they were hunkered down to defy melting until at least the summer solstice. I could tell the AECL summer students had not yet arrived, because the water tower did not yet say "Beer River." There's now a traffic light on the highway where it intersects with Deep River Road, right where you cross over to the Elms Hotel (now called the Bears Den, no apostrophe), which no longer has a "Ladies and Escorts" entrance, and serves a South Asian buffet instead of chuck wagon sandwiches of dubious provenance. But if I squint my eyes just the right way, I can see the DRW on the shoulder of the highway, walking back from the dairy, wearing jeans so wide and long that we look like hovercrafts when we walk, feet black with water buffalo sandal dye, laughing about something only teenagers would find funny. Wishing we were nowhere near this place.

Acknowledgements

Big thanks to my King's College mentors, Charlotte Gill, Harry Thurston, and Cooper Lee Bombardier, and my ongoing gratitude to my class of 2020 cohort for their insightful feedback, indignant commiseration, and intelligent discourse.

CPSIA information can be obtained
at www.ICGtesting.com
Printed in the USA
LVHW041937191020
669186LV00018B/413